The Madcap Giant Book of Jokes

The Madcap Giant Book of Jokes

Gyles Brandreth

Illustrated by David Farris

MADCAP

Published in Great Britain in 1997 by Madcap Books, André Deutsch Ltd, 106 Great Russell Street, London, WC1B 3LJ. André Deutsch Ltd is a subsidiary of VCI plc

Text copyright © 1997 Madcap Books/Gyles Brandreth
Illustrations copyright © David Farris

A catalogue record for this title is available from the British Library

ISBN 0 233 99192 1

Cover illustrations by Andy Hammond

All rights reserved. This book is sold subject to the condition that it may not be reproduced, stored in a retrieval system, or transmitted, in any form or by any means, electronic, mechanical, photocopying, recording or otherwise, without the publisher's prior consent.

Printed by Vincenzo Bona, Italy

CONTENTS

How to be Funny	8	Jokes Jokes Jokes Jokes Jokes Jokes	50
The A–Z of Jokes	12	Dressing up/Making up	52
Do-it-yourself Apple-Pie Bed	16	Play For Today	53
Crazy Graffiti	17	Comedy with Class	58
Cartoon Cavalcade	18	Elephant Jokes	60
Mad Games	20	Giraffe Jokes	61
Loony Limericks	22	Dotty Doodles	62
Food Glorious Food!	24	Terrible Tonguetwisters	63
Crazy I.Q. Test	25	Emergency Jokes	65
How to be a Ventriloquist	26	The Mad Hatter's Tea Party	68
How to make a Ventriloquist Dummy	26	Ads Gone Wrong	70
Science for Beginners	28	Shaggy Dog Stories	72
The Complete Practical Joker	29	Magnificent Misprints	74
Animal Magic	32	Confucius, He Say	76
Doctor, Doctor!	33	The Daffy Dictionary	77
Join the Circus	34	Verse – and Worse	80
April Foolery	36	Meet the Super Heroes	81
Masterriddle	37	Meet the Monsters	82
Hilarious Howlers	40	Crazy Puzzles	84
Crazy Challenges	42	Waiter, Waiter!	86
Signs of the Times	44	Car Signs	87
Knock Knock	46	The Haunted House	88
A Page of Poetry	48	Brandreth's Bookshelf	90
Cartoon Corner	49	The 100 Worst Jokes in the History of the World	91

HARD CHEESE

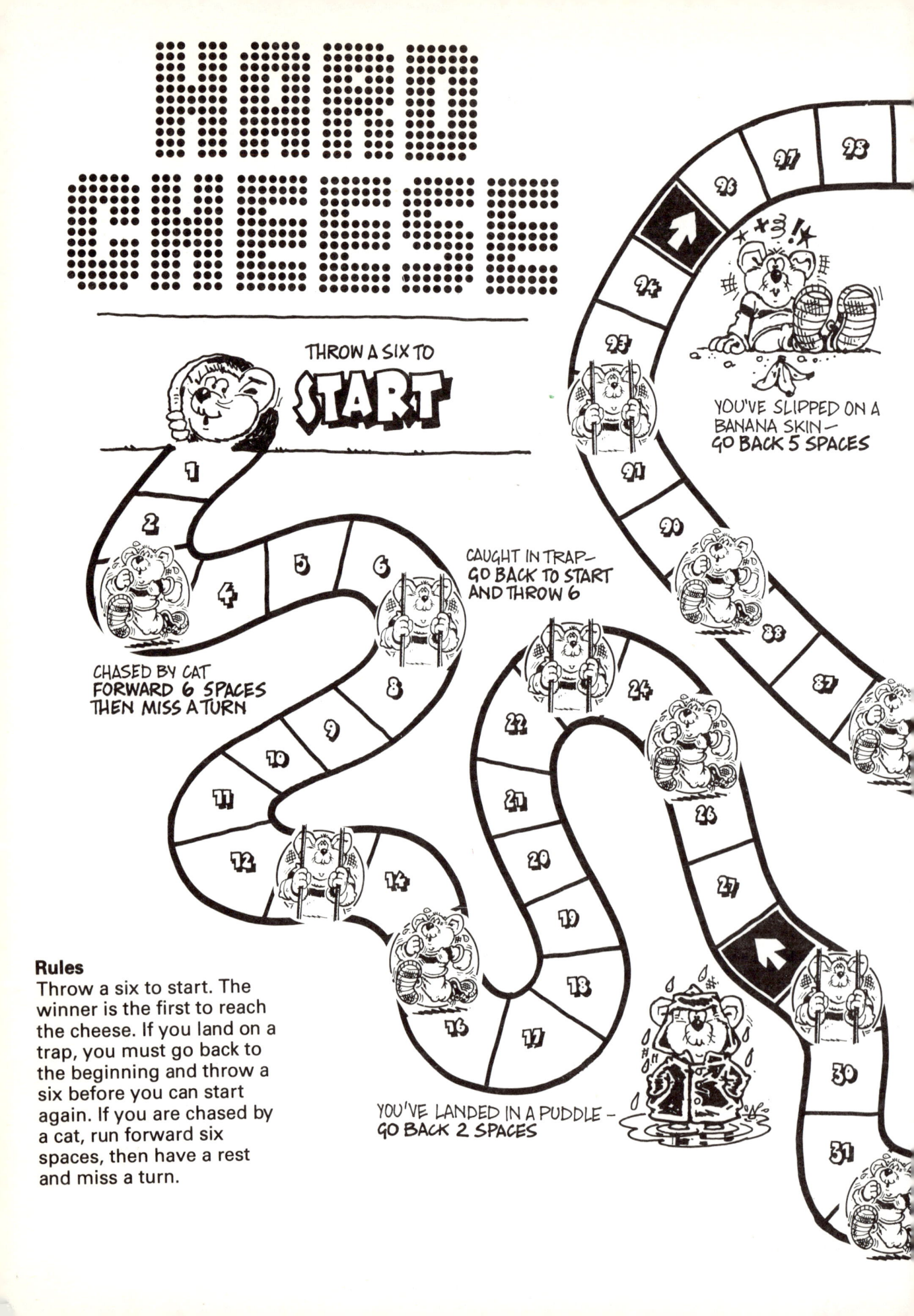

THROW A SIX TO **START**

YOU'VE SLIPPED ON A BANANA SKIN — GO BACK 5 SPACES

CAUGHT IN TRAP — GO BACK TO START AND THROW 6

CHASED BY CAT FORWARD 6 SPACES THEN MISS A TURN

YOU'VE LANDED IN A PUDDLE — GO BACK 2 SPACES

Rules
Throw a six to start. The winner is the first to reach the cheese. If you land on a trap, you must go back to the beginning and throw a six before you can start again. If you are chased by a cat, run forward six spaces, then have a rest and miss a turn.

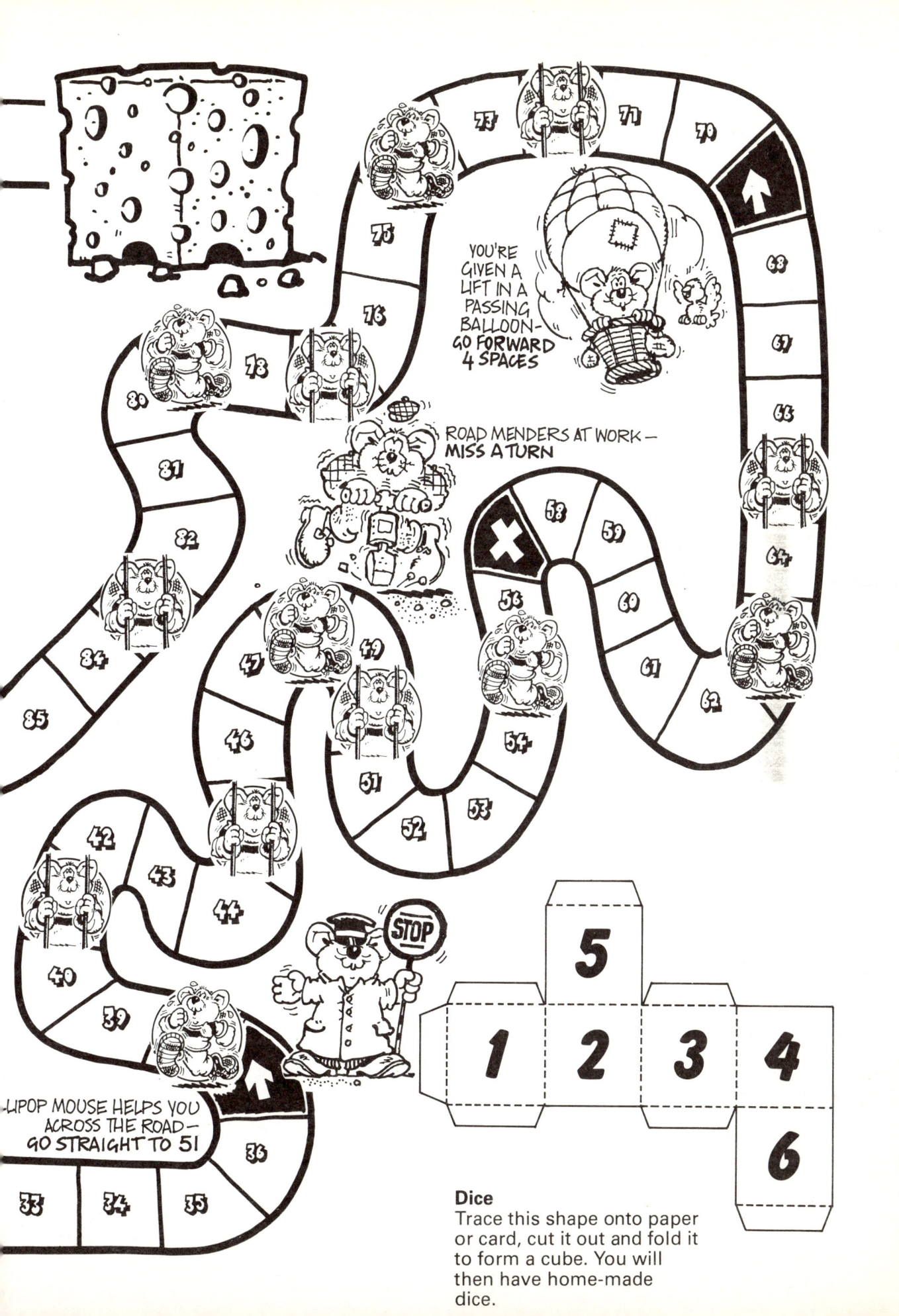

YOU'RE GIVEN A LIFT IN A PASSING BALLOON— GO FORWARD 4 SPACES

ROAD MENDERS AT WORK — MISS A TURN

LOLLIPOP MOUSE HELPS YOU ACROSS THE ROAD — GO STRAIGHT TO 51

Dice
Trace this shape onto paper or card, cut it out and fold it to form a cube. You will then have home-made dice.

HOW TO BE FUNNY

Everyone can be funny and there are so many different ways in which you can make people laugh. Here are some of the best ways to be funny:

1. *You can tell jokes*

Try this one out on your friends—
 'Did you know they're not going to grow bananas any longer?'
 'No, why?'
 'Because they're long enough already!'

2. *You can recite crazy poems*

There was a young lady from Gloucester,
Whose parents thought they had lost her.
 From the fridge came a sound
 And at last she was found.
The problem was – how to defrost her.

3. *You can fool your friends*

Take a piece of paper and write the word WHAT on it. Put the piece of paper in your pocket and say to your friend: 'I know what you are going to say next.' Your friend is certain to ask 'What?' and you can then produce your piece of paper and say: 'There! I told you I knew what you would say!'

4. *You can pull a funny face*

Place your two index fingers in the corners of your mouth and pull them to give yourself a very wide grin. Now stick out your tongue as far as it will go, and try and look at the tip of your nose at the same time! The funny face you make will have your friends in stitches – but don't pull your mouth too hard or you'll find you need stitches too!

5. You can play a silly game

Try the *Laughing Game*. Get someone to sit on a chair and look as serious and straight-faced as they can. They must try to remain serious while you make every attempt to get them laughing. Pull funny faces, tell jokes, and keep at it until the person laughs, then you can change places.

6. You can tell some riddles

What is the biggest ant of all?
  An eleph-ant.
What can you touch, see and make, but can't hold?
  Your shadow.

7. You can play practical jokes

Take some extra strong glue and a 5p or 10p coin and glue it to the pavement. All you have to do now is hide and watch passers-by try to pick it up!

8. You can do silly walks

Swing each leg as far forwards and backwards as it will go when you walk, and wave your arms up and down as you stride along.

9. *You can do animal impressions*

Hide under a bed or in a cupboard until someone comes into the room and then, when they least expect it, make a noise like an elephant trumpeting or a pig grunting. You could also play a game by making animal noises and getting your friends to guess what they are.

10. *You can wear funny clothes*

Dressing up in your parents' clothes is always fun, but try walking into a room wearing a ridiculous hat or a really large pair of trousers. Take care to keep a very serious face, just as if the clothes you are wearing are perfectly normal. Put a shirt and tie on back to front and people will think your head has twisted round the wrong way!

11. *You can tell Knock-Knock jokes*

Knock-knock.
  Who's there?
Atch.
  Atch who?
Use your hankie when you sneeze!

12. *You can do impersonations of your friends*

Study your friends and see if they have any particular mannerisms, such as a very distinctive walk, or some characteristic by which you can recognize them, and see if you can copy it. Be kind in your mimicry, however. It isn't funny to upset your friends!

13. *You can use silly voices*

Place your tongue over your *bottom* teeth and keep it there. Now try to speak. You'll find you've got a very funny voice. Try curling your tongue upwards too and press it against the roof of your mouth and speak. Your friends will be in hysterics, especially if you talk to them over the telephone.

14. *You can make funny noises*

Blow up a balloon and then let the air out again very slowly. It makes a marvellous noise. Make noises yourself too. For example, try copying the sound a bath makes as the water disappears down the plughole!

15. *You can do magic tricks*

The funniest tricks are those that go wrong, so drop your pack of cards on the floor as you shuffle them. Tell people that you are going to pull a chicken out of a hat and pull out an egg or a feather instead, telling them the chicken has vanished!

BET YOU CAN'T MAKE ME LAUGH.

11

The A-Z of Jokes

A

ACCIDENT
A lorry carrying treacle has collided with a car on the M6. Police are advising motorists to stick to their own lanes.

ASTRONAUT
Why are astronauts successful people?
Because they always go up in the world.

B

BANANA
What do you do with a blue banana?
Try and cheer it up.

BRICK
Why is a brick like an egg?
Because it has to be laid.

C

CANNIBALS
What do cannibals play at parties?
Swallow my leader.

CHESS
'My dog plays chess with me.'
'He must be very clever.'
'Not really. I've won four games out of five already.'

D

DEPARTMENT STORE
Customer: I'd like a fur coat for my wife.
Assistant: I'm sorry, sir, but we don't do exchanges.

DIETING
The simplest way to diet is to get lockjaw.

E

ELECTRICIAN
What did the electrician's wife say when he was late home from work?
'Wire you insulate?'

EXCUSES
'The telephone is ringing. Why don't you answer it?'
'Why should I? I don't know who's calling.'

FLIES
How do you keep flies out of the kitchen?
Put a bucket of manure in the lounge.

FOOTBALL
'If I hadn't been in goal we'd have lost 20–nil.'
'Oh? What was the score then?'
'Nineteen–nil!'

GHERKIN
What's green and holds up stagecoaches?
Dick Gherkin.

GRANDMA
Grandma: I wouldn't slide down the banister like that if I were you.
Tracy: Oh, how would you slide down, Grandma?

HORN
What did the broken car horn say?
'I don't give a hoot.'

HYPOCHONDRIA
Did you hear about the hypochondriac who was so full of drugs that if he sneezed in the direction of a sick person he cured them.

IDOL
'My mum treats me like an idol.'
'Oh, why?'
'She gives me burnt offerings for meals.'

INVENTORS
Teacher: Who was the greatest inventor of all time?
Pupil: Edison. He invented the phonograph and the radio so that we would sit up all night and use his lightbulb.

JAIL
1st Prisoner: Why are you in here?
2nd Prisoner: Because I trod on a nail. It just happened to be in a policeman's shoe.

JOBS
Why did the angel lose his job?
Because of harp failure.

KANGAROO
Why did the mother kangaroo scold her children?
Because they ate biscuits in bed.

KNIFE
Did you hear about the doctor who lost his patients?
He kept sticking the knife in.

LIFE SPAN
What has the shortest life span in the world?
A New Year's resolution. It's born before midnight, and is dead and forgotten the next day.

LOONY
Why did the loony bait his hook with mice when he went fishing?
Because he wanted to catch cat fish.

METERS
Benjamin Franklin may have invented electricity, but it was the man who invented the meter that made all the money.

MOVIES
Mark: Excuse me, can you tell me if this movie is very long?
Timothy: Long? The intermission is in August.

NOUGAT
Common Clara: Would you like some nougat?
Stuck-up Sarah: It's pronounced nouga. The T is silent.
Common Clara: Not the way you drink it!

OPTIMIST
Sally: What is an optimist?
Gloria: It's a woman who buys small steaks and doesn't think they'll shrivel when she cooks them.

OVERWEIGHT
Did you hear about the overweight man who took a shower?
He didn't get his feet wet.

PARROT
What do you get if you cross a parrot with a woodpecker?
A bird that knocks on doors and delivers messages.

PETRIFIED
Teacher: How does a tree become petrified?
Pupil: The wind makes it rock.

QUEEN
Why did the Queen's son cry a lot?
Because he was the Prince of Wails.

QUESTIONS
What never asks questions but gets plenty of answers?
A doorbell.

RAINCOAT
'My raincoat has a waterproof label.'
'Pity that the whole coat isn't waterproof.'

REPORTER
Newspaper reporter: My editor sent me to do the burglary.
Policeman: You're too late, it's already been done.

SANDWICH
Why did the boy call his dog 'sandwich'?
Because he was half-bred.

SERGEANT
'I don't think the drill sergeant likes me.'
'Why not?'
'He was training us in how to throw a hand grenade, and he told me to hold the grenade between my teeth and throw away the pin.'

T

TAIL
Why is getting up at four o'clock in the morning like a pig's tail?
Because it's twirly (too early).

TRAFFIC WARDEN
What do traffic wardens have in their sandwiches?
Traffic jam.

U

U.F.O.
Barry: The restaurant around the corner does a fantastic U.F.O. meal.
Harry: What's a U.F.O. meal?
Barry: An Unidentified Frying Object.

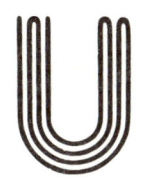

UGLINESS
Did you hear about the girl who was so ugly that Boy Scouts used to whistle at her as their good deed for the day.

V

VEGETARIAN
What do vegetarian cannibals eat?
Swedes.

VISITING
Molly: We visited the cemetery today.
Dolly: Oh, somebody died?
Molly: Yes, all of them.

W

WIND
What did the north wind say to the east wind?
'Let's play draughts.'

X

XPLANATIONS
Teacher: Can you explain to me the difference between a barber in ancient Rome and an excited circus owner?
Pupil: Yes, miss. One is a shaving Roman and the other is a raving showman.

Y

YORICK
What was Yorick's nickname at school?
Numbskull.

Z

ZOO
Handsome Horace: Why are you buying two tickets?
Ugly Eric: One to get into the zoo, and one to get out.

ZEBRA
What do you get if you cross a zebra with a pig?
Striped sausages.

I DON'T GET THE JOKE!

DO IT YOURSELF

APPLE PIE BED

Making an apple-pie bed is easy when you know how.
Here's how to do it:

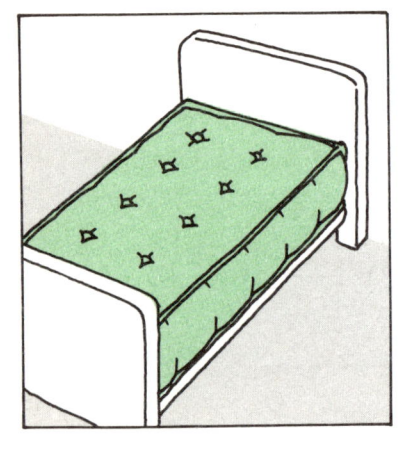

1. Take all the sheets and blankets off your victim's bed.

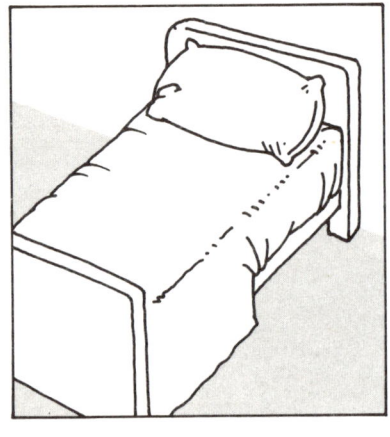

2. Put on the bottom sheet, but only tuck it in at the top.

3. Fold the bottom sheet back up so that it hangs loosely over the top half you've already tucked in.

4. Don't bother about a second sheet, you won't need one. Now put the blankets on as usual, tucking them in all round.

5. Finally fold the untucked end of the sheet back over the top of the blankets and it will *look* like the top end of the sheet that isn't there!

6. Now the bed looks perfectly normal, until of course your victim tries to get in it. He will only be able to put his feet in a few centimetres!

"How do I like school?— CLOSED."

"If I survive this, can I have some sweets?"

"How much longer is she going to be? I'm expecting a call from Sitting Bull!"

GENTS HAIRDRESSER
CLOSED

FOOT PATH

I HATE Cartoon

GIVE ANTS A BREAK—

YOU CAN ALWAYS COUNT ON YOUR FINGERS

Our needlework teacher is a real sew and sew!

William Tell wore contact lenses.

GIVE KARATE THE CHOP.

WHAT IS THE HARDEST THING TO DO? milk puddings

YOU CAN ALWAYS COUNT ON YOUR FINGERS

I HATE GRAFFITI
I hate all foreign food

WALK ON ONE LEG

I'm the biggest liar in the World!
— I DON'T BELIEVE YOU

LEGALISE TELEPATHY!
— I knew you were going to say that!

LIGHTNING NEVER STRIKES twice in the same place.
— NO, IF IT STRIKES ONCE, THE SAME PLACE ISN'T THERE ANY MORE!

HYPOCHONDRIACS MAKE ME SICK.

DOWN WITH GRAVITY

MAD GAMES

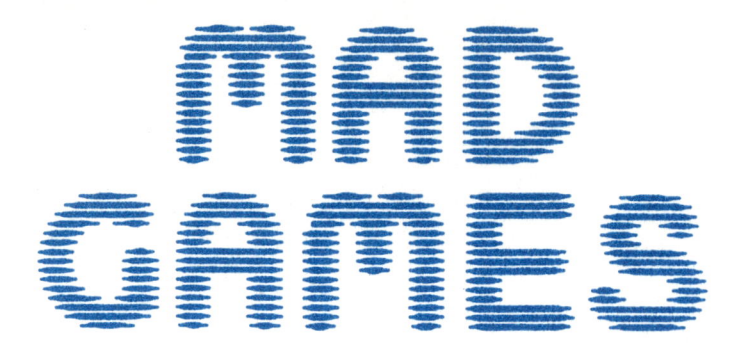

Fanning the Kipper

Cut some 'kipper' shapes out of tissue paper and give one to each of the players, together with a magazine or comic. Place a row of plates at one end of the room and get the players to stand at the other end with their kipper on the floor in front of them. On the shout of 'Go!' each player must fan his or her kipper with the magazine, and waft it towards the plate. The winner is the first person to get a kipper onto their plate, without touching the kipper either with their hands or the magazine.

Pass the Orange

Stand your players in a circle. One player places an orange under his chin. The orange must then be passed from chin to chin around the circle. If anyone touches the orange with their hands or drops it they must leave the ring. The winner is the last player left.

Knock Knees

This game is similar to 'pass the orange', except the players pass a balloon by holding it between their knees. If anyone drops the balloon they must leave the circle, and the winner is the person left with the balloon when everyone else is out.

The Picture Frame Game

This hilarious game is quite simple to set up. All you need is an old picture frame, and some friends. Hold the frame up to your face so that you are framed. Then, without laughing or smiling, try to look like a portrait in a gallery. The more serious you look, the more your friends will laugh. If you laugh too, one of the other players should take your place.

Sausages

For some unknown reason, the word SAUSAGES always makes people laugh. The object of this game is to try *not* to laugh. One person acts as a questioner (who is allowed to laugh), and asks each person in turn a question. Whatever the question is – What do you hang on a Christmas tree? – Where do flies go in winter? – What is your favourite pet? – the person answering it must reply 'sausages'. The first player to laugh then becomes the questioner.

Ankle Guessing

Get some of your friends to lie on the floor and cover them with a blanket so that only their feet and ankles stick out. The rest of your friends must then take a piece of paper and a pencil and write down whose ankles are sticking out and the order in which they appear.

Silly Shopping

All the players sit in a circle. You begin by saying: 'On Saturday I went to the supermarket and bought three baboons.'

The next player will then add on his purchase saying: 'On Saturday I went to the supermarket and bought three baboons and a packet of custard powder.'

The next adds on his purchase: 'On Saturday I went to the supermarket and bought three baboons, a packet of custard powder, and some hair curlers.'

So the game continues, building up the list, until someone forgets one of the purchases and is disqualified. The winner is the last one left.

Apple-Ducking

This is a very old game and is especially fun on Hallowe'en. Simply get a large bowl of water and float some apples on the top. The players must then put their hands behind their back and pick the apples out of the water *with their teeth*.

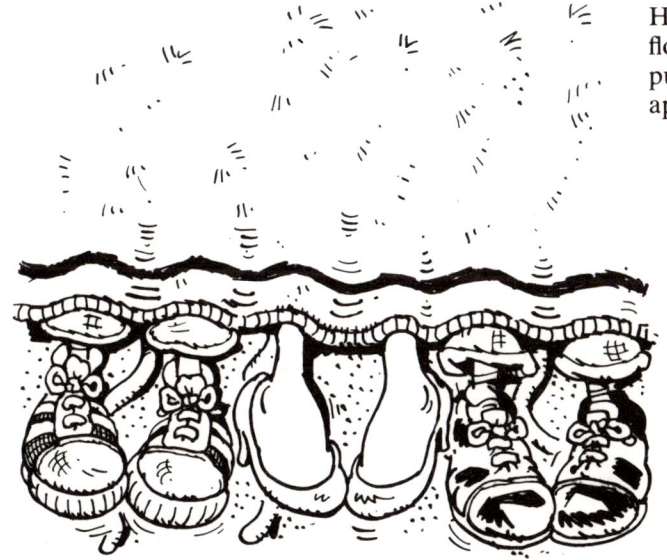

A jovial fellow named Packer
pulled a joke out from a cracker.
It said: 'If you're stuck
for a turkey, try duck —
you could say it's a real Christmas quacker!'

A bow-legged policeman from Kew
said: 'I really don't know what to do.
I can stop without fuss
a lorry or bus,
but mini-cars simply go through.'

A sleeper from the Amazon
put nighties of his grandma's on.
The reason? That
he was too fat
to get his own pajamazon.

There was an old lady of Worcester
who was kept awake by a rooster
so she cut off his head
and made sure he was dead
and now he can't crow like he use-ter.

A girl we know, Doris de Fleet,
is so unusually neat.
She washes all day
to keep microbes away
and wears rubber gloves just to eat.

There was a young lady of Lynn,
who was so uncommonly thin,
that when she essayed
to drink lemonade,
she slipped through the straw and fell in.

LOONY LIMERICKS

A PROFESSOR NAMED AUBREY BRETT
SAID, 'THREE THINGS I ALWAYS FORGET.
THERE'S ALL MY FRIENDS' NAMES,
AND THE TIMES OF MY TRAINS,
AND THE THIRD ONE I CAN'T RECALL YET.'

THERE ONCE WAS A LADY FROM EALING
WHO JUST COULDN'T STOP HERSELF SQUEALING.
SHE SQUEALED TO THE CAT
WHO TRIPPED OVER THE MAT
AND THE SCAR ON ITS HEAD IS NOW HEALING.

A SAFE-CRACKING THIEF CALLED MCBRIDE
ONCE BLEW A SAFE-DOOR OPEN WIDE.
WHEN THE DUST CLEARED AWAY,
HE WAS FILLED WITH DISMAY,
FOR HE FOUND THERE WAS NOTHING INSIDE.

THERE WAS A YOUNG LADY NAMED PERKINS,
WHO WAS SO VERY FOND OF GHERKINS.
ONE DAY AT TEA
SHE ATE FIFTY-THREE,
AND PICKLED HER INTERNAL WORKINGS.

THERE WAS A YOUNG LADY NAMED ROSE
WHO HAD A BIG WART ON HER NOSE.
WHEN SHE HAD IT REMOVED
HER APPEARANCE IMPROVED
BUT HER GLASSES SLIPPED DOWN TO HER TOES.

I HATE POETRY!

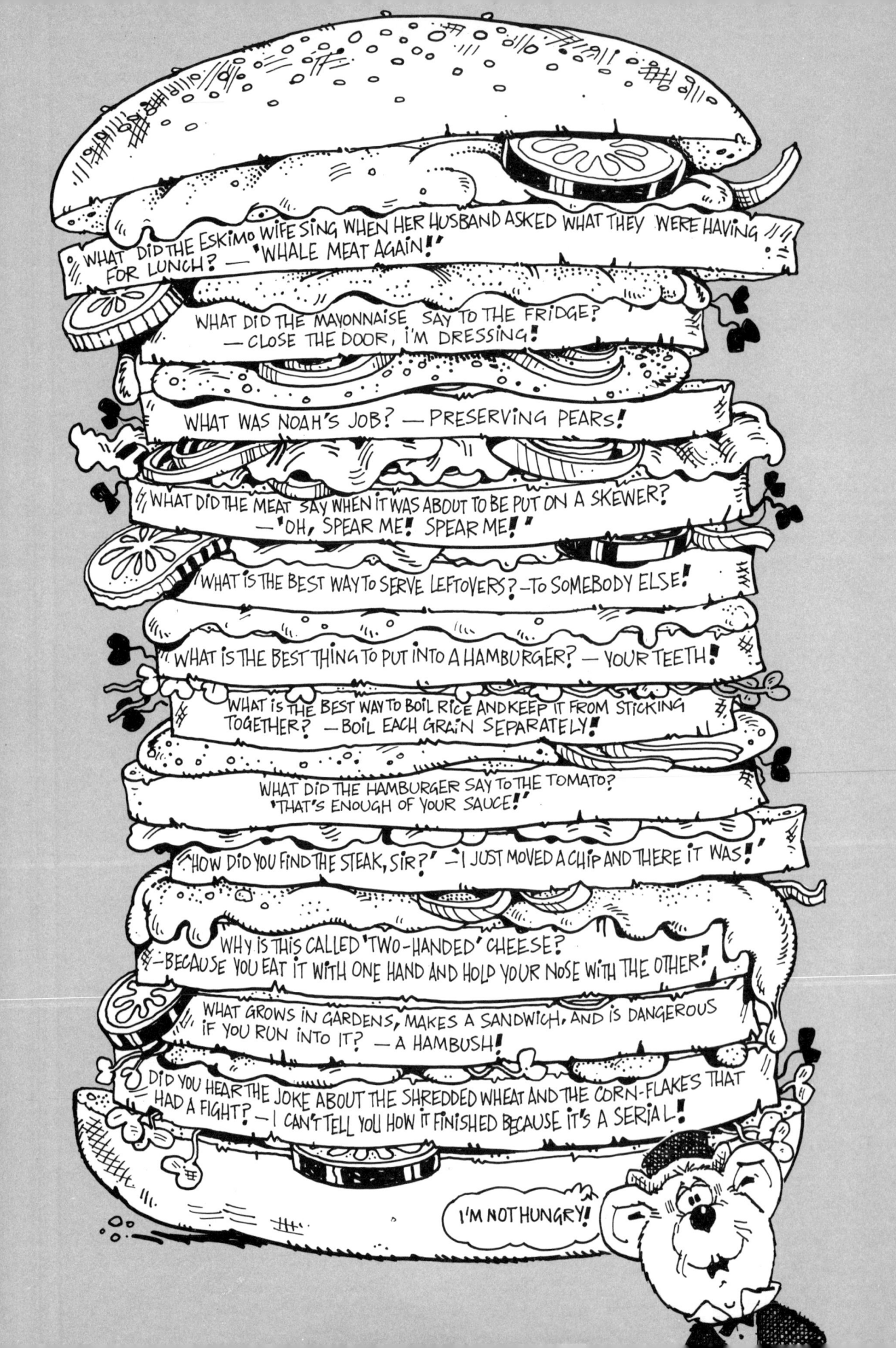

WHAT DID THE ESKIMO WIFE SING WHEN HER HUSBAND ASKED WHAT THEY WERE HAVING FOR LUNCH? — "WHALE MEAT AGAIN!"

WHAT DID THE MAYONNAISE SAY TO THE FRIDGE? — CLOSE THE DOOR, I'M DRESSING!

WHAT WAS NOAH'S JOB? — PRESERVING PEARS!

WHAT DID THE MEAT SAY WHEN IT WAS ABOUT TO BE PUT ON A SKEWER? — "OH, SPEAR ME! SPEAR ME!"

WHAT IS THE BEST WAY TO SERVE LEFTOVERS? — TO SOMEBODY ELSE!

WHAT IS THE BEST THING TO PUT INTO A HAMBURGER? — YOUR TEETH!

WHAT IS THE BEST WAY TO BOIL RICE AND KEEP IT FROM STICKING TOGETHER? — BOIL EACH GRAIN SEPARATELY!

WHAT DID THE HAMBURGER SAY TO THE TOMATO? 'THAT'S ENOUGH OF YOUR SAUCE!'

"HOW DID YOU FIND THE STEAK, SIR?" — I JUST MOVED A CHIP AND THERE IT WAS!

WHY IS THIS CALLED 'TWO-HANDED' CHEESE? — BECAUSE YOU EAT IT WITH ONE HAND AND HOLD YOUR NOSE WITH THE OTHER!

WHAT GROWS IN GARDENS, MAKES A SANDWICH, AND IS DANGEROUS IF YOU RUN INTO IT? — A HAMBUSH!

DID YOU HEAR THE JOKE ABOUT THE SHREDDED WHEAT AND THE CORN-FLAKES THAT HAD A FIGHT? — I CAN'T TELL YOU HOW IT FINISHED BECAUSE IT'S A SERIAL!

I'M NOT HUNGRY!

CRAZY I.Q. TEST

I.Q. stands for 'Intelligence Quotient'. An I.Q. test is designed to show how intelligent you are. See how many of the questions you can answer below:

1. What colour is a red bus? ....

2. How long is a piece of string? ....

3. If a red house is made of red bricks, and a blue house is made of blue bricks, what is a green house made of? ....

4. How far is it (in kilometres) from London to the capital city of England?

5. Who invented the wheel? ....

6. At what age were you born? ....

7. How do you spell ANTICLERICALISM?

8. If you have 100 eggs in a basket, how many do you have? ....

9. How deep is a hole? ....

10. Dick Turpin's horse was called 'Black Magic'. True or false? ....

11. Whose last words were 'I don't know why they're selling this corned beef at 20p a tin...'? ....

12. How can you dilute water? ....

13. Who painted the Mona Lisa? Beatrix Potter/Luke Skywalker/ Julius Caesar/Leonardo Da Vinci..........

14. What day of the week was the day before the day after yesterday? ....

15. What is a baby dog called: a kitten/a piglet/or a puppy? ....

16. If a tree fell down at night one hundred miles from the nearest person, would there be any sound? ....

17. What does the smell of roses look like?

18. How did Queen Elizabeth I travel to London? On a no. 64 bus/on a bike/in a Jumbo Jet/by horse and carriage ....

19. What language do Russians speak?..........

20. Do hands grow on palm trees? ....

You will find the answers on page 99. If you scored at least 10 points you should be at university. If you scored 11 or more, you are a genius. Congratulations!

25

How to be a Ventriloquist

A ventriloquist is a person who has learnt to speak without making his lips move, so that it looks as if his puppet, or 'dummy' as it is called, is speaking. The best ventriloquists are so convincing that people really believe the dummy can speak. You too can be a ventriloquist, but it takes a lot of practice. Here are a few tips:

1. Sit in front of a mirror and try to speak without moving your lips. You will find it easier if you do not close your mouth tightly, but keep your lips slightly apart.

2. Practise taking slow, deep breaths in and out as you speak, and you will feel that it makes a difference to your voice. If you breathe out as you speak your voice will become much louder. This is called 'throwing' your voice, and makes it appear that the voice is coming from elsewhere and not from you.

3. Have a conversation with yourself, speaking first normally as yourself, and then answering in your ventriloquist's voice, with your lips closed. It will come easily after practice.

4. Now try saying the letters of the alphabet without moving your lips. You will find that the letters 'b', 'f', 'm', 'p' and 'v' are the most difficult, but they can be said by pressing the tongue against the roof of your mouth at the same time.

5. The letter 'v' can be substituted for 'b', so that if you have to say 'bottle of beer' you say 'vottle of veer'. With practice you can make it sound like a proper 'b'.

6. Try to avoid using words that contain the letters 'p' and 'm' as these are particularly difficult to say.

Practise your art in front of a mirror.

Keep your lips slightly apart.

If you cannot master the technique of ventriloquism and find it impossible – don't worry! If you cannot do it well, do it badly! Some of the funniest ventriloquist acts are when the dummy's head falls off, or the mouth moves at the wrong time, or the ventriloquist turns his head away so that the audience cannot see his lips move. A very entertaining sketch can be performed in this way and should have your audience in hysterics!

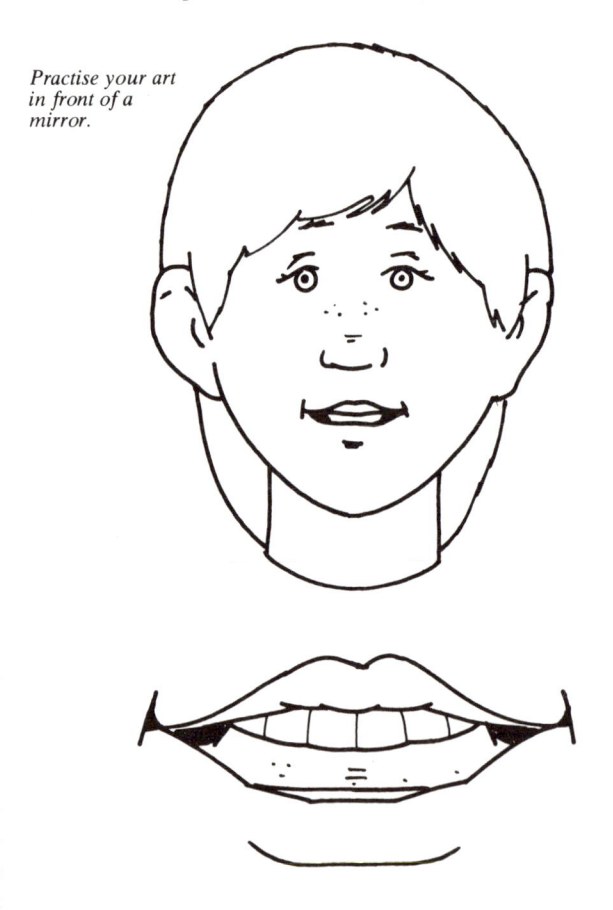

HOW TO BECOME A VENTRILOQUIST IN 2 MINUTES!

Yes, there is a way of becoming a ventriloquist in a very short time. The answer is to CHEAT! You can sit on a table with your dummy on your knee and have a conversation with it, and no one will see your lips move when the dummy speaks. Why? Because you have a friend hidden under the table who does the dummy's voice! You can work out a very funny script beforehand, and you will be hailed as the world's greatest ventriloquist. Do make sure that your friend remains out of sight throughout.

If you're going to cheat, make sure there's not a dog about!

HOW TO MAKE A VENTRILOQUIST'S DUMMY

Your hand makes a good dummy.

Professional ventriloquists have very expensive dummies, often made of wood, sometimes with moving eyes as well as a moving mouth. These work by a series of levers or strings inside. But you do not need anything as complicated or expensive. Here are some cheap ideas for dummies:

1. The cheapest of all is the 'naked dummy' – your hand. Clench your fist. Tuck your thumb under your fingers. Now move your thumb up and down and you will see that it looks like a mouth. Stick two pieces of gummed paper onto your hand for eyes, and using your mother's lipstick (ask her first!) you can draw lips on your hand too.

2. If you have an old sock you can slip it over your hand and put your fingers in the same position as above. The advantage of a sock is that you can sew buttons on for eyes, wool for hair, draw a nose on with a felt tipped pen, and create your own character.

3. Get a friend (preferably a small friend!) to act as your dummy. Put two red dots on his or her face to look like rosy cheeks, and draw a line from each corner of the mouth going downwards to make it look like a wooden dummy. Your 'dummy' can then sit on your knee like a proper dummy – and talk too!

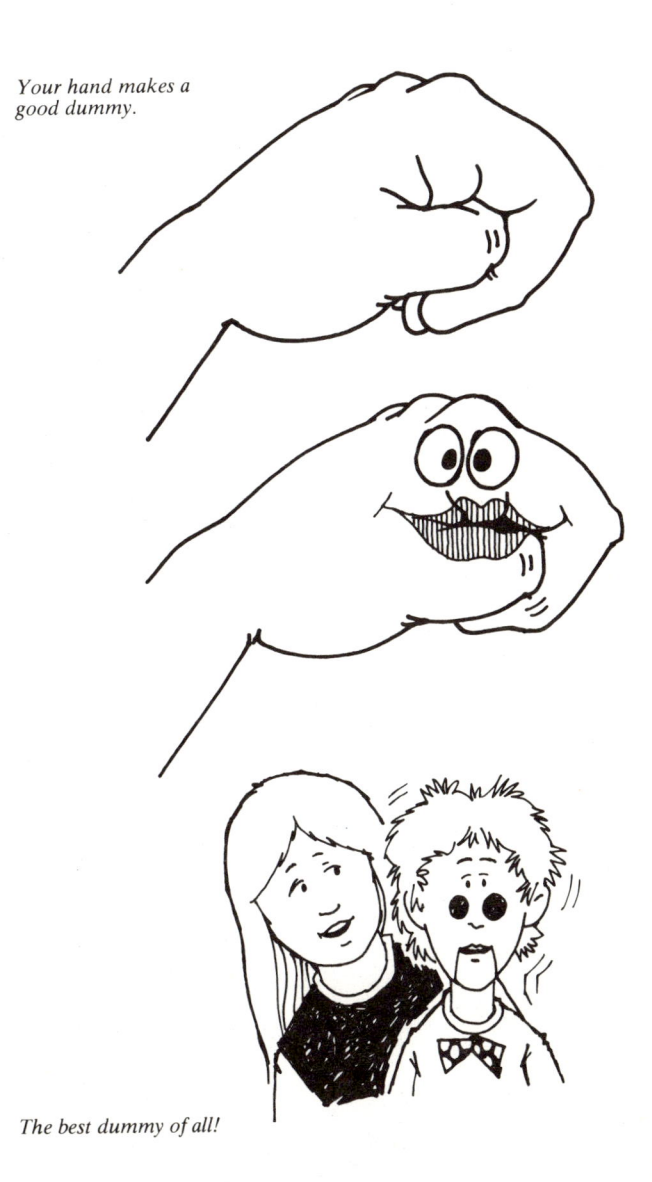

The best dummy of all!

Science for Beginners

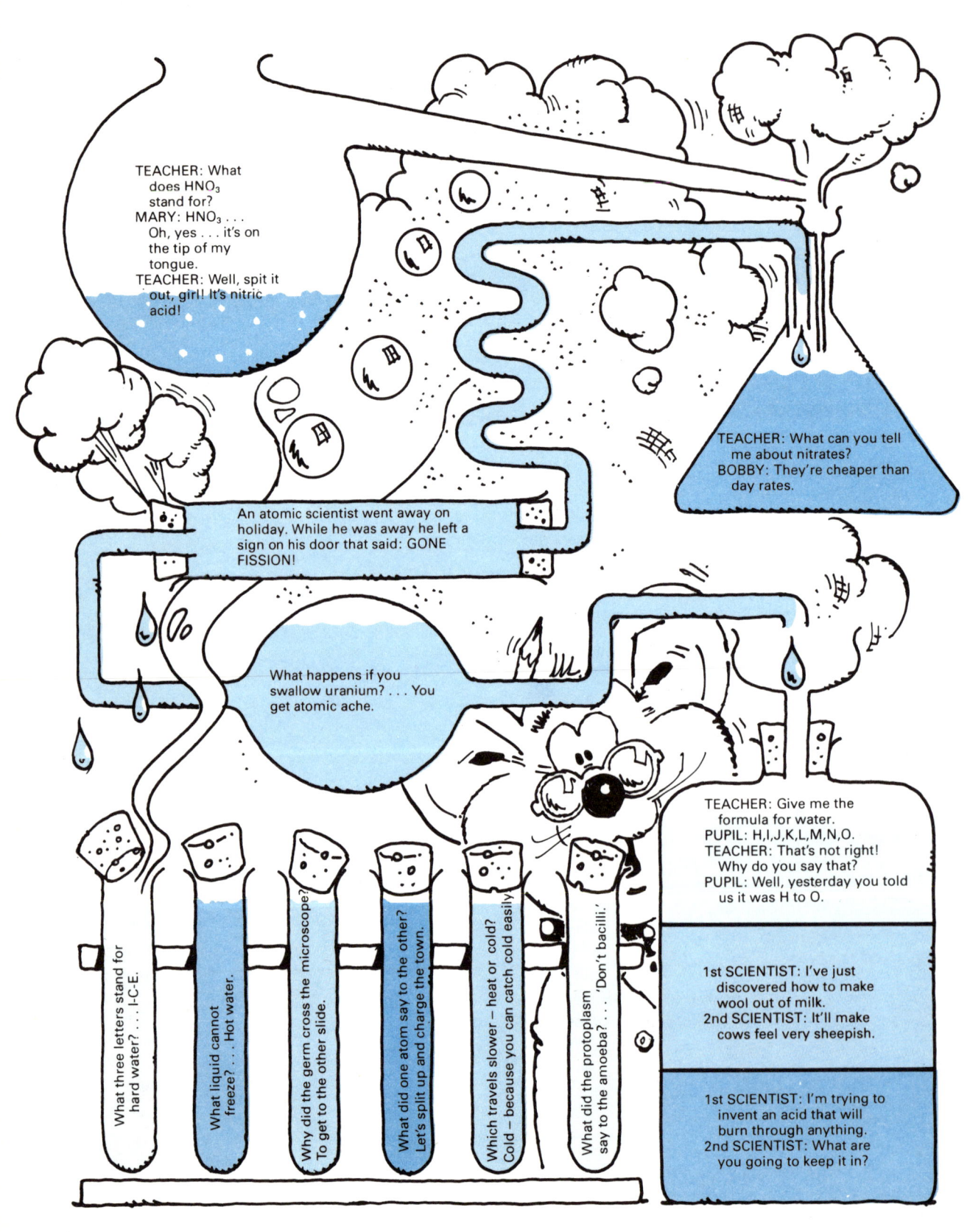

TEACHER: What does HNO₃ stand for?
MARY: HNO₃... Oh, yes... it's on the tip of my tongue.
TEACHER: Well, spit it out, girl! It's nitric acid!

TEACHER: What can you tell me about nitrates?
BOBBY: They're cheaper than day rates.

An atomic scientist went away on holiday. While he was away he left a sign on his door that said: GONE FISSION!

What happens if you swallow uranium?... You get atomic ache.

TEACHER: Give me the formula for water.
PUPIL: H,I,J,K,L,M,N,O.
TEACHER: That's not right! Why do you say that?
PUPIL: Well, yesterday you told us it was H to O.

1st SCIENTIST: I've just discovered how to make wool out of milk.
2nd SCIENTIST: It'll make cows feel very sheepish.

1st SCIENTIST: I'm trying to invent an acid that will burn through anything.
2nd SCIENTIST: What are you going to keep it in?

What three letters stand for hard water?... I-C-E.

What liquid cannot freeze?... Hot water.

Why did the germ cross the microscope? To get to the other slide.

What did one atom say to the other? Let's split up and charge the town.

Which travels slower – heat or cold? Cold – because you can catch cold easily.

What did the protoplasm say to the amoeba?... 'Don't bacilli.'

The Complete PRACTICAL JOKER

When planning practical jokes take care that you are not going to frighten or upset your victims, especially if they happen to be old or frail. Only play practical jokes on people who you *know* will laugh at your joke, otherwise the joke might be on you.

Dotty Joke
Say to your friend: 'Here's a piece of paper and a pencil. I want you to write a small letter I with a dot over it.'

Of course, your victim will think that this is easy and is certain to write 'i' on the paper, which is wrong! A small letter I with a dot over it looks like this: i.

Cactus Caper
This is an excellent joke with which to fool your teacher. Tell your teacher that your mother has a new hobby: she is growing cacti, and has grown a unique specimen. The next day you take in this rare plant as a very special present. In fact it is a scouring pad in a pot of real earth, but unless your teacher is an expert he or she could look after this unique plant for years!

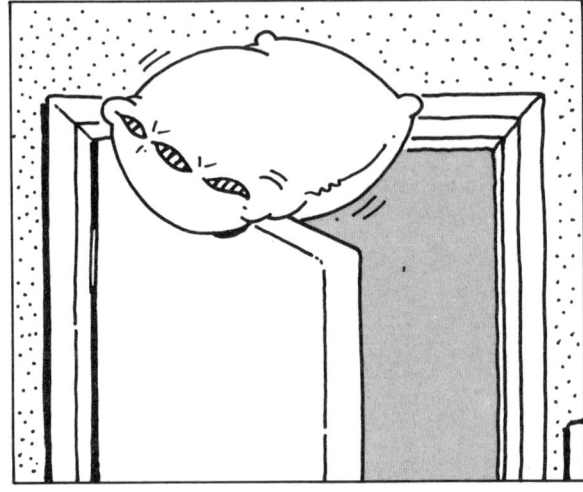

Cactus Caper

Pillow Power
This is one of the oldest, but still one of the funniest, practical jokes of all time. Simply balance a pillow on the top of a door that is slightly ajar, and when the victim walks in the pillow will hit him on the head. Don't use anything heavier than a pillow.

Pillow Power

What's Up?
Stand in the street with a friend and point upwards towards the sky. Keep looking up and before long you will be joined by a crowd!

What's up?

Pyjama Tops

All you need for this joke is some cotton and a needle. Take someone's pyjamas or nightdress and put a few stitches either in the sleeves or the legs, so that when your victim attempts to put them on, they will find they can't get their arm or leg through. You will have a good laugh as they wriggle about trying to get inside – but don't sew them up too tightly or they'll never make it!

Eggspertise

Next time you have boiled eggs for breakfast collect all the empty eggshells, secretly of course, wash them carefully and hide them until you want to use them. One morning you can offer to cook the breakfast. All you need to do is cook one egg for yourself, and in the other egg-cups you put your empty shells upside down so that they look like real eggs. When the family arrive you can be eating your delicious egg, but they'll have a big surprise when they crack theirs open and find nothing inside!

Eggspertise

Practical Presents

At Christmas time or for a friend's birthday you can give a lovely present wrapped in beautiful paper – the bigger the parcel the better. When your friend opens the parcel there will be another parcel inside it. Inside that will be another parcel, and another and another. Make sure there are at least TEN layers of wrapping. In the centre will be an old potato! When your friend (if you are still friends!) has waded through this lot, you can then hand over your real present.

Golden Handshake

Next time you meet friends, be sure to shake hands with them, and watch the expression on their faces. In the palm of your hand you will have a spoonful of honey or jam!

Stick Up

Take the inside pages from an old newspaper and glue them all together. When they are nicely stuck and it is quite impossible to open any of the pages, place them inside the front pages of TODAY'S paper. Now watch what happens when someone attempts to read the paper and wonders why they can't open the pages!

Round the Bend

This is a very funny joke. All you need is a long ball of string, or a very long tape measure. Stand outside a building, stop a passer-by and tell him you are measuring the building. Having asked for his help, get him to hold one end of the string while you walk off round the other side of the building, unravelling the string as you go. Once you are around the corner, find another victim and give him the other end of the string to hold.

Leave both your victims standing where they are and go to a spot where you can observe them but they can't see you. See how long it is before they start to investigate and discover who is on the other end of the string!

Round the Bend

ANIMAL MAGIC

What did one kangaroo say to another kangaroo during a thunderstorm? 'I wish it would stop raining – I hate to have my kid cooped up like this.'

What do you give a pig with a sore throat? Oinkment.

What happens when a frog's van breaks down? It gets toad away.

What did the horse say when he got to the end of his nosebag? 'This is the last straw.'

What do you call a howling baby whale? A little blubber.

How do you find a lost rabbit? Make a noise like a carrot.

Why did the baby porcupine say 'Is that you, Mum?' Because he backed into a cactus.

What is green and highly dangerous? A caterpillar with a gun.

'I'm going to keep this skunk under my bed.' 'But what about the smell?' 'Oh, he'll just have to get used to it.'

What animal has two humps and is found at the North Pole? A lost camel.

What is the hardest part about milking a hamster? Getting a bucket under it.

A mouse fell off a wall. What did the other mouse do? He used mouse-to-mouse resuscitation.

Why did the lion cross the road? Because it was the chicken's day off.

Why does a chicken watch television? For hentertainment.

Who went into a tiger's den and came out alive? The tiger.

What do you do if a gorilla decides to sleep in your bed? Sleep somewhere else.

What do polar bears have for lunch? Ice burgers.

What is green and slimy and goes hith? A snake with a lisp.

1st RHINOCEROS: What's that over there?
2nd RHINOCEROS: It's a hippopotamus.
1st RHINOCEROS: Fancy having such an ugly face!

Why are pelicans expensive to feed? Because of their large bills.

DOCTOR, DOCTOR!

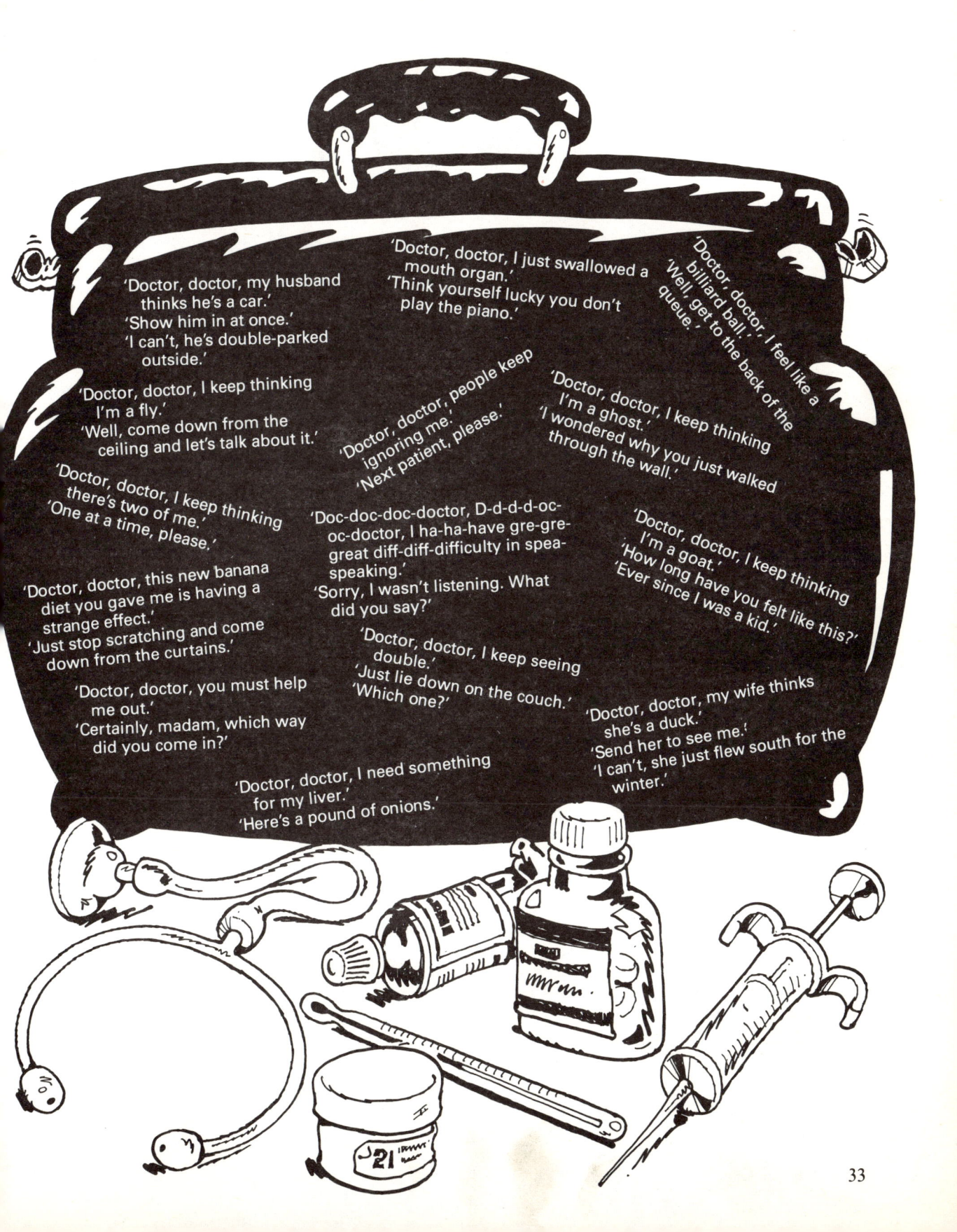

'Doctor, doctor, my husband thinks he's a car.'
'Show him in at once.'
'I can't, he's double-parked outside.'

'Doctor, doctor, I just swallowed a mouth organ.'
'Think yourself lucky you don't play the piano.'

'Doctor, doctor, I feel like a billiard ball.'
'Well, get to the back of the queue.'

'Doctor, doctor, I keep thinking I'm a fly.'
'Well, come down from the ceiling and let's talk about it.'

'Doctor, doctor, people keep ignoring me.'
'Next patient, please.'

'Doctor, doctor, I keep thinking I'm a ghost.'
'I wondered why you just walked through the wall.'

'Doctor, doctor, I keep thinking there's two of me.'
'One at a time, please.'

'Doc-doc-doc-doctor, D-d-d-d-oc-oc-doctor, I ha-ha-have gre-gre-great diff-diff-difficulty in spea-speaking.'
'Sorry, I wasn't listening. What did you say?'

'Doctor, doctor, I keep thinking I'm a goat.'
'How long have you felt like this?'
'Ever since I was a kid.'

'Doctor, doctor, this new banana diet you gave me is having a strange effect.'
'Just stop scratching and come down from the curtains.'

'Doctor, doctor, I keep seeing double.'
'Just lie down on the couch.'
'Which one?'

'Doctor, doctor, you must help me out.'
'Certainly, madam, which way did you come in?'

'Doctor, doctor, my wife thinks she's a duck.'
'Send her to see me.'
'I can't, she just flew south for the winter.'

'Doctor, doctor, I need something for my liver.'
'Here's a pound of onions.'

I'M A JUMBO JET
I LEFT THE CIRCUS... I WAS TIRED OF WORKING FOR PEANUTS!
TIGHT-ROPE WALKERS ARE JUST LIKE BOOK-KEEPERS— WE HAVE TO KEEP OUR BALANCE!
STOP ACTING THE FOOL!
WHAT IS THE DIFFERENCE BETWEEN AN ACROBAT AND A DUCK?
ONE GOES QUICK ON HER LEGS—THE OTHER GOES QUACK ON HER LEGS!
LET'S TAKE MAURICE TO THE CIRCUS—!
IF THEY WANT HIM LET THEM COME AND GET HIM!
WE REGRET TO ANNOUNCE THAT THE INVISIBLE MAN WILL NOT BE SEEN TONIGHT!
LAST NIGHT I DREAMT I'D EATEN A 200 KILO MARSHMALLOW!
DON'T WORRY, IT WAS ONLY A DREAM.
YES, BUT WHEN I WOKE UP MY PILLOW WAS GONE!
WHAT HAPPENED TO THE MAN WHO WORKED AS A HUMAN CANONBALL?
OH, HE'S BEEN DISCHARGED!

I'VE GOT A CLEVER CAT— IT EATS CHEESE AND BREATHES DOWN MOUSEHOLES WITH BAITED BREATH!
I'M ON MY WAY TO BURY ST. EDMUNDS...
WHY? IS HE DEAD?
I'M NOT ACTING!
ONE OF MY LIONS SWALLOWED A LIGHT BULB LAST NIGHT...
IS HE ALRIGHT NOW?
YES, HE'S FINE. HE SPAT IT OUT THIS MORNING, AND NOW HE'S DE-LIGHTED!
I'M SO STRONG I CAN TEAR UP A TELEPHONE DIRECTORY!
SO WHAT? I CAN TEAR UP A STREET!
HOW DID YOU GET THIS JOB?
I JUST PULLED A FEW STRINGS!
WHAT HAPPENED TO THE GIRL YOU USED TO SAW IN HALF?
SHE'S NOW LIVING IN MANCHESTER AND LONDON!

1 APRIL

What a Question!
If you really want to fool your mother say to her: 'Mum, why did you drop that £5 note into the rubbish bin?' The result will be a lot of scrabbling and frantic searching as she empties the rubbish bin all over the kitchen floor, looking for the £5 note. After about ten minutes you return and shout: APRIL FOOL!

I Spied a Spider
Shout and scream: 'Aaaaaarrrggghhh! There's a horrible great big hairy spider over there! It's enormous!' Everyone in the room will leap on to the table screaming and shouting: 'Help! Where is it?' After a couple of minutes you shout: APRIL FOOLS!

Thread Bare
All you need for this joke is a reel of cotton and a needle. Thread the needle with cotton and push the end of the cotton through your jacket so that just a couple of centimetres are lying on your shoulder. You can keep the rest of the cotton on the reel in your inside pocket. Before long someone will see the little bit of cotton on your shoulder and try to remove it. As soon as they take hold of the loose end you walk away as fast as you can, leaving your victim with a piece of cotton that is getting longer and longer and l-o-n-g-e-r.

Take Notice
On a piece of paper write a message, such as 'Please Kiss Me', and attach it to someone's back with a piece of sticky tape. You can do this without them noticing by giving them a friendly pat on the back as you greet them. All day long they will walk around with the sign on their back and wonder why they are suddenly so popular!

Give a Ring
Take a piece of sticky tape and place it over the receiver rest on your telephone (under the receiver) so that it stays down when the receiver is lifted. The next time the telephone rings and someone answers it, they will lift the receiver and be amazed when the phone continues ringing!

'Hello, and welcome to "Masterriddle", the special quiz game in which we are looking for the person who can answer the most riddles in the country. The champion will receive the much acclaimed title of MASTERRIDDLER!'

1. What's the route through the Khyber called? — Pass.

2. How do you dance in Saudi Arabia? — Sheik-to-Sheik.

3. What do people always cry over? — Onions.

4. Why was the bill-poster sacked? — Because he couldn't stick at the job.

5. What is the wife of an engineer called? — Bridget.

6. What did Noah say when he heard the rain come down? — Ark!

7. What happened when the cat swallowed a penny? — There was some money in the kitty.

8. What is the difference between here and there? — The letter T.

9. What is all over the house? — The roof.

10. Where do all good turkeys go when they die? — To oven.

11. What did they call Carrie the porter? — Carrie the bag.

12. What did they call Baxter the bricklayer? — Baxter the Wall.

13. Make one word from the letters in NEW DOOR. — One word.

14. Why do Irish farmers wear capes? — To cape them warm.

15. What was the largest island before Australia was discovered? — Australia.

16. Why did the gardener throw roses into the burning building? — Because flowers grow better in hot houses.

17. How many letters are there in the alphabet? — Eleven. T-H-E A-L-P-H-A-B-E-T.

18. What would a cockerel do if it lost its knees? — Go to London where the Cockneys are.

19. What is a copy-cat? — An artist painting a self-portrait.

20. What did one sheep say to the other sheep at the gate? — After ewe.

21. Why can't ducks fly upside down? — Because they would quack up.

38

22. What has four legs and can fly? — Two birds.

23. Which bird can lift the heaviest weight? — The crane.

24. If cheese comes after dinner, what comes after cheese? — A mouse.

25. Which is the house without a mouse? — A snail's house.

26. How do you keep cool at a football match? — Sit next to a fan.

27. What paper does a cat read on a Sunday? — The Mews of the World.

28. What did the inventor of carpets make? — A pile.

29. If a boy should lose a knee where does he go to get another one? — To a butcher's where kid-ney's are sold.

30. Why is it not safe to sleep on a train? — Because trains run over sleepers.

31. Can a match box? — No, but a tin can.

32. If crocodile skins make good shoes, what do banana skins make? — Good slippers.

33. What did the Leaning Tower of Pisa say to Big Ben? — If you've got the time, I've got the inclination.

34. What is the best way to hunt bear? — With your clothes off.

35. When is it correct to say 'I is'? — 'I is the letter after H.'

36. Which animals are poor dancers? — Four-legged ones, because they have two left feet.

37. What did Santa Claus' wife say during a thunderstorm? — 'Come and look at the rain, dear.'

38. How do you make a ham roll? — Push it.

39. What can a whole apple do that half an apple can't? — It can look round.

40. What was the lawyer's wife called? — Sue.

41. How many birds can you put in an empty cage? — One — after that it isn't empty.

42. How can you say 'I am looking for you' in three letters? — I-C-Q.

39

- A hostage is a nice lady on an aeroplane.

The Gorgons had long snakes in their hair and looked like women, only more horrible.

The Sewage Canal is in Egypt.

A Goatee is a miniature Goat.

A Blizzard is the inside of a chicken.

The smallest wind instrument is the Picadilly.

People who test your eyes are called Optimists.

A Medicine Ball is a Dance for Sick Animals.

VANDALS ARE OPEN-TOED SANDALS WORN BY ANCIENT ROMANS.

VENISON IS A CITY IN ITALY WITH LOTS OF CANALS.

Florence Nightingale was a famous Swedish Soprano.

Livid was a famous Roman Poet.

Margarine is made from imitation cows.

A CENTURION IS A ROMAN WHO IS A HUNDRED YEARS OLD.

The Pope lives in the vacuum.

MAGNETS ARE LITTLE CREATURES FOUND IN ROTTEN APPLES.

A Spatula is the bone behind your shoulder blade.

Moths eat hardly nothing, except holes.

HANDEL WAS A SMALL BOY IN A STORY BY GRIMM AND HAD A SISTER CALLED GRISTLE.

CONSERVATION IS WHEN YOU TALK TO PEOPLE.

Macaroni invented the radio.

Boxers sometimes give each other a paunch on the nose.

TUNISIA IS A DISEASE WHERE YOU LOSE YOUR MEMORY.

CLEOPATRA DIED FROM A BITE OF a WASP.

a Centimetre is an insect with a hundred legs.

An oxygen haz eight sides.

Alligator shoes are made from crocodile skin.

JACOB HAD A BROTHER CALLED SEE-SAW.

The Second Wife of Henry VIII was Anne Berlin.

Monsoon is a French word meaning Mister.

A Doggerel is a little Dog.

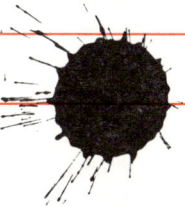

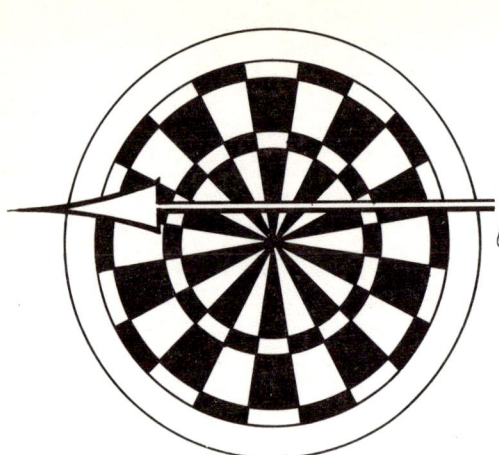

CRAZY CHALLENGES

Orange Juice
For this challenge you will need three oranges. Take the first orange and see if you can balance it on your forehead. Tip your head back to look at the ceiling to do this . . . See if you can balance it there for one minute.

When you have perfected this, try balancing two oranges on your head at the same time. In Birmingham there is an eleven-year-old boy who can balance three oranges on his head for 92 minutes, which is a world record! You may not be able to balance three for that long, but count for how many seconds you can balance three oranges on your head before they roll off.

Penny Problem
Take ten 20p coins or 5p's if you are not rich enough to have ten 20p's. Leave your left hand palm downwards on the table, place one coin on each finger (between the nail and the knuckle) and balance them there. When you have five coins on your left hand the challenge is to get the other five coins on to your right hand, *without* any of the coins falling off. You should end up with one coin balanced on each finger.

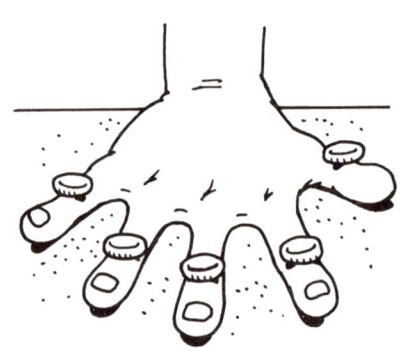

A-Peeling!
Next time you have an apple try to peel it so that all the peel comes off in one long piece and you end up with one long spiral of peel. Some clever adults can cut an apple peel very carefully and thinly so that they end up with a strip several metres long. Take great care not to cut yourself in the process.

Everyday Noises
This challenge can be played as a game. Below are a list of everyday sounds. What you have to do is imitate those noises with your voice, tongue and teeth as accurately as you can. Your friends must guess what the noises are. If they guess correctly, you'll have the proof that you were making the right sounds!

Here are the noises to imitate:

1. A telephone dialling.
2. A car starting.
3. A baby crying.
4. A grandfather clock ticking.
5. A vacuum cleaner.
6. Gas escaping.
7. A steam train.
8. A door creaking.
9. A clock being wound up.
10. Footsteps on a country road.

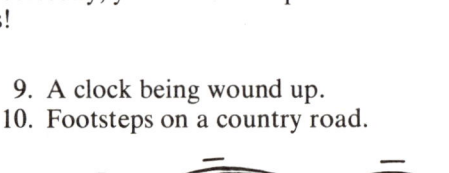

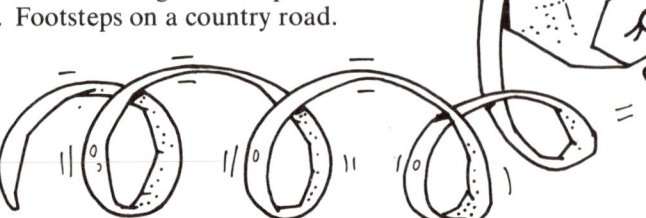

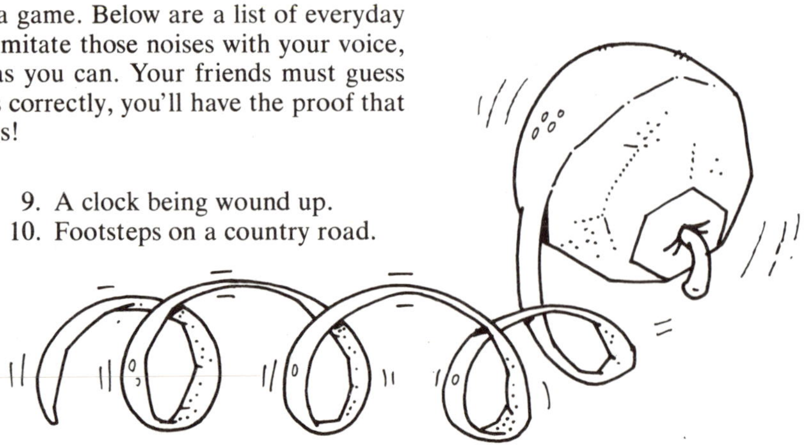

Happy Challenge

This challenge can be undertaken on a journey and will prove how many happy people there are in the country. As you travel along in a car, pick out a person at the side of the road, give them a big smile and wave to them as you drive past. The challenge is to do it so nicely that they smile back.

Smile, rather than grin, otherwise they will think you are laughing *at* them and will feel offended. If you are with a friend, you can see who can collect the most smiles.

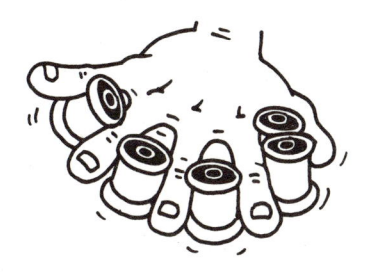

Pick it Up

Collect as many cotton reels as you can for this challenge. Put two between your thumb and first finger and pick them up. Then add a third, a fourth, and so on. The challenge is to see how many you can pick up. Challenge your friends to see who can pick up the most.

Blind as a Bat

Take a pencil and paper, and a scarf. Blindfold yourself and make sure you cannot see anything at all. And no cheating by peeping! With the pencil in your hand, draw four squares, one at a time. Draw them on top of each other as if they were a pile. When you've finished, take off the blindfold and see how well you've done.

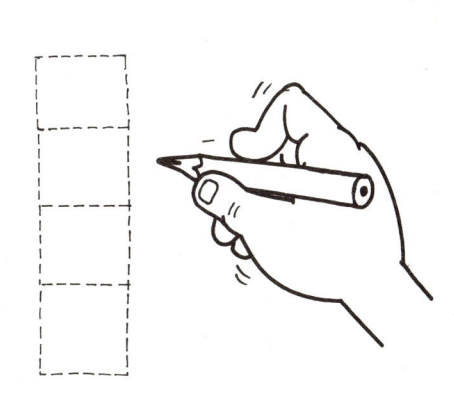

Bloated Balloons

This is a messy challenge and must only be done outside.

You will need:
1. Some balloons.
2. Some water.
3. Some old waterproof clothes.
4. Some very good friends.

Fill a balloon with half a litre or so of warm water, depending on the size of the balloon, and tie it at the top. You will now have a nice squelchy ball. Get your friends to stand in a circle and throw the balloon from one to another. You must keep it in the air, because if you drop it the balloon will burst and cover you in water. The challenge is to keep the balloon whole, and yourselves dry!

← COOPERATIVE FAMILY BUTCHERS

RESTAURANT 34

POLLUTION is a Dirty Word

CUSTOMERS WHO FIND OUR STAFF RUDE SHOULD WAIT AND SEE THE MANAGERESS.

WE SERVE SUNDAY LUNCHES SEVEN DAYS A WEEK.

CLOSED

LUNCHES WILL BE SERVED FROM 11:30 UNTIL THE END OF OCTOBER.

EARS PIERCED WHILE YOU WAIT

WOMAN WANTED TO RUN UP CURTAINS

HORSE MANURE

A FILLED BAG: 40p
DO-IT-YOURSELF: 20p

NO CHILDREN ALOUD

Will the individual who borrowed a ladder from the Caretaker kindly return it immediately or further steps will be taken.

WET PAINT
WATCH IT OR WEAR IT

YOUR FEET ARE KILLING ME

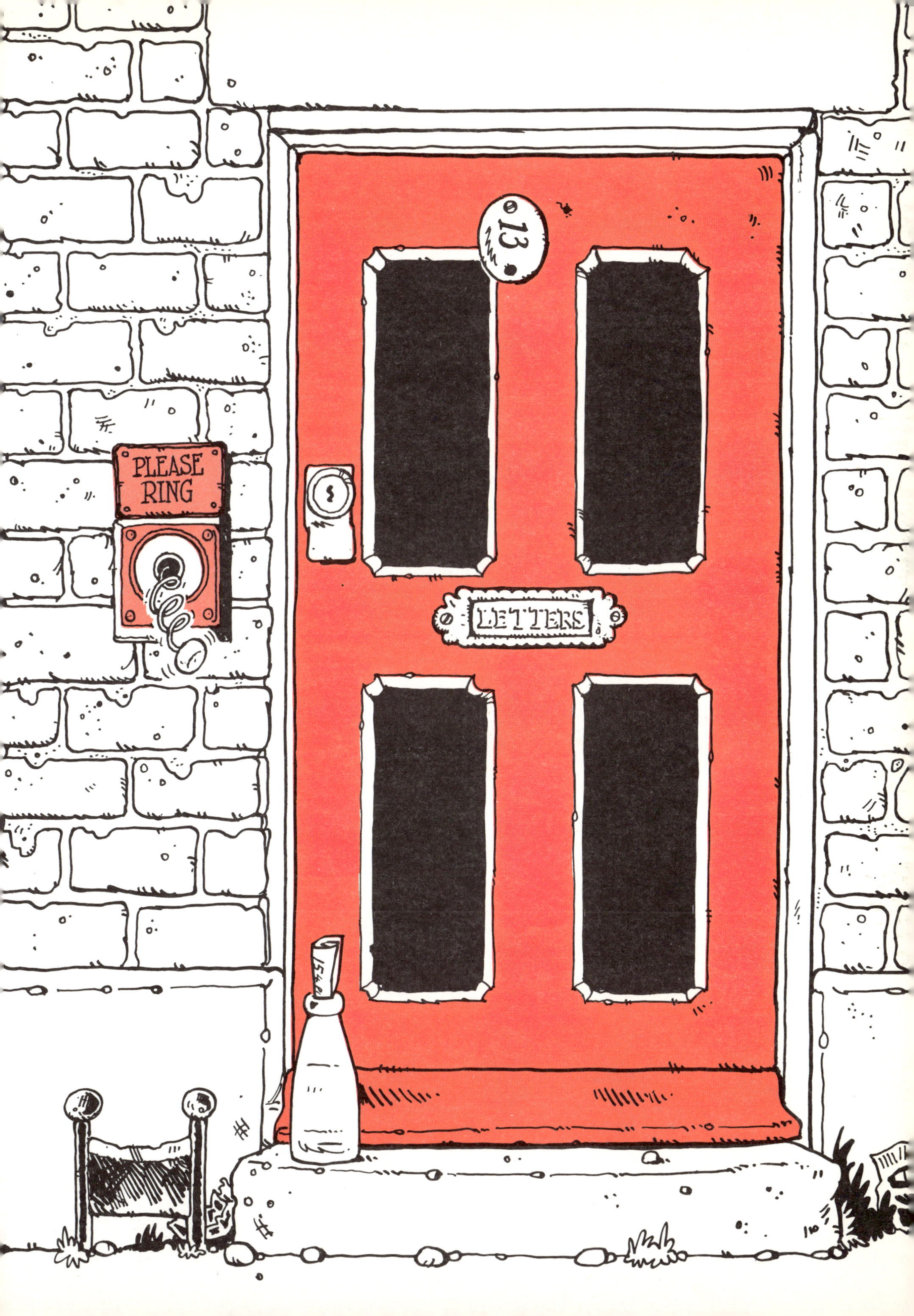

13
PLEASE RING
LETTERS

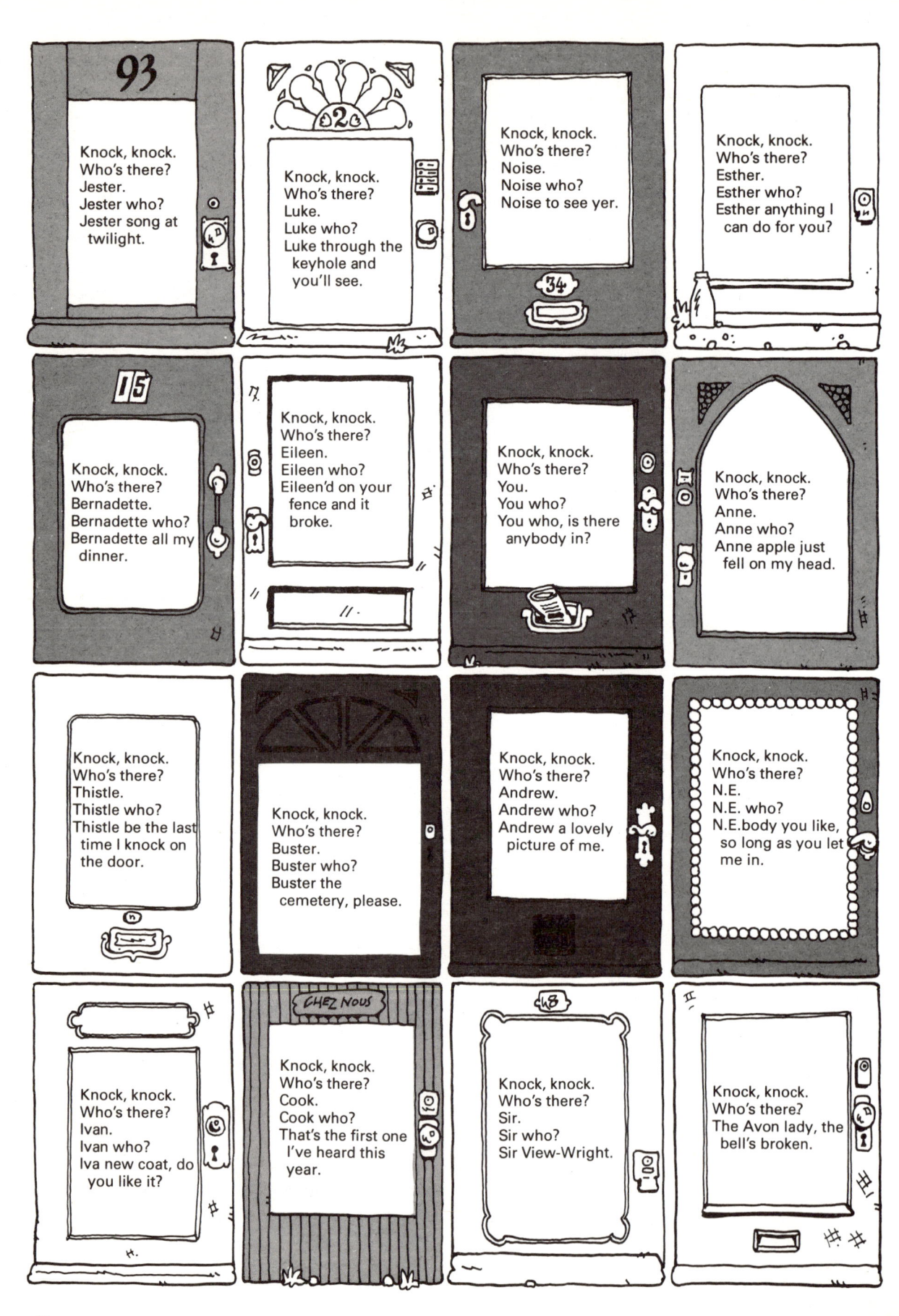

Knock, knock.
Who's there?
Jester.
Jester who?
Jester song at twilight.

Knock, knock.
Who's there?
Luke.
Luke who?
Luke through the keyhole and you'll see.

Knock, knock.
Who's there?
Noise.
Noise who?
Noise to see yer.

Knock, knock.
Who's there?
Esther.
Esther who?
Esther anything I can do for you?

Knock, knock.
Who's there?
Bernadette.
Bernadette who?
Bernadette all my dinner.

Knock, knock.
Who's there?
Eileen.
Eileen who?
Eileen'd on your fence and it broke.

Knock, knock.
Who's there?
You.
You who?
You who, is there anybody in?

Knock, knock.
Who's there?
Anne.
Anne who?
Anne apple just fell on my head.

Knock, knock.
Who's there?
Thistle.
Thistle who?
Thistle be the last time I knock on the door.

Knock, knock.
Who's there?
Buster.
Buster who?
Buster the cemetery, please.

Knock, knock.
Who's there?
Andrew.
Andrew who?
Andrew a lovely picture of me.

Knock, knock.
Who's there?
N.E.
N.E. who?
N.E. body you like, so long as you let me in.

Knock, knock.
Who's there?
Ivan.
Ivan who?
Iva new coat, do you like it?

Knock, knock.
Who's there?
Cook.
Cook who?
That's the first one I've heard this year.

Knock, knock.
Who's there?
Sir.
Sir who?
Sir View-Wright.

Knock, knock.
Who's there?
The Avon lady, the bell's broken.

Knock, knock.
Who's there?
Sari.
Sari who?
Sari I was sarong.

Knock, knock.
Who's there?
Pop.
Pop who?
Pop over to the shop for me.

Knock, knock.
Who's there?
Willoughby.
Willoughby who?
Willoughby quick and open the door.

Knock, knock.
Who's there?
Phyllis.
Phyllis who?
Phyllis glass up with water.

Knock, knock.
Who's there?
Don.
Don who?
Don mess about, open the door.

Knock, knock.
Who's there?
Tish.
Tish who?
Sorry you've got a cold.

Knock, knock.
Who's there?
Jupiter.
Jupiter who?
Jupiter hurry or you'll miss the bus.

Knock, knock.
Who's there?
Buddha.
Buddha who?
Buddha this piece of bread for me.

Knock, knock.
Who's there?
Mary.
Mary who?
Mary in haste, repent at leisure.

Knock, knock.
Who's there?
Butcher.
Butcher who?
Butcher left leg in, your left leg out . . .

Knock, knock.
Who's there?
Europe.
Europe who?
Europe early this morning.

Knock, knock.
Who's there?
Shelby.
Shelby who?
Shelby coming round the mountain when she comes.

Knock, knock.
Who's there?
Sacha.
Sacha who?
Sacha lot of questions.

Knock, knock.
Who's there?
Ivor.
Ivor who?
Ivor terrible cold.

Knock, knock.
Who's there?
Boo.
Boo who?
Don't start crying again.

OOOPS!

47

A Page of Poetry

Jack and Jill went up the hill,
To fetch a pail of water.
Jack fell down and broke his crown,
And sued the farmer and his daughter.

'Twas in a restaurant they met,
Romeo and Juliet.
He had no cash to pay the debt
So Romeo'd what Juliet.

Newton heard a sort of plonk –
An apple fell upon his conk;
Discovered gravitation law;
It shook old Isaac to the core.

'Your teeth are like the stars,' he said,
And pressed her hand so white.
He spoke the truth, for like the stars,
Her teeth came out at night.

Sweet little Eileen Rose
Was tired and sought some sweet repose.
But her sister Clare
Put a pin on her chair
And sweet little Eileen rose!

A dog is loved
  By old and young.
He wags his tail
  And not his tongue.

I'M FAIRLY GRACIOUS TO THE BORE
   WHO TELLS ME JOKES I'VE HEARD BEFORE,
BUT HE WILL FIND ME GLUM AND GRIM
   WHO TELLS ME JOKES I TOLD TO HIM!

"All together now—'for he's a jolly good fellow!'"
"I never knew you could yodel, Bert!"
"I suppose you'll be wanting chips as well?"
Stop fighting in there.
"Oops sorry,... wrong apple."
AAAHHAAAAAAA
"Sounds as though Tarzan has got cramp again."
CHEMIST
DISPENSARY
"Gentleman complaining about a prescription you made up for him."
DO NOT TOUCH THE EXHIBITS
MOUSE NEWS

JOKESJOKESJOKES JOKESJO

What means of transportation gives people colds? A choo-choo train. / On which side does a chicken have the most feathers? On the outside. / What is a myth? A lady with a lisp but no husband. / Your sister has got big ears! From the back she looks like a loving cup! / Why was Cinderella thrown out of the hockey team? Because she ran away from the ball. / What happens to old horses? They become nags. / When an old Red Indian called Short Cake died, his tribe argued about who should dig the grave. In the end his wife settled it. She said, 'Squaw bury Short Cake.' / 'Mummy, mummy, all the kids say I look like a werewolf.' 'Shut up and comb your face.' / What comes after the letter A? All of them. / What do you call a man whose job is inspecting rabbit holes? A burrow surveyor. / How do we know that Moses wore a wig? Because sometimes he was seen with Aaron and sometimes without. / What does the sea say to the sand? Nothing, it just waves. / What is a cow's favourite TV programme? Dr Moo. / Why did Little Bo Peep lose her sheep? Because she had a crook with her. / What word minus a letter makes you sick? Music. / Where do elves go to get fit? To an Elf Farm. / What is red, runs on wheels, and eats grass? A bus. P.S. I lied about the grass. / 'Not only have you broken my heart and ruined my entire life by breaking off our engagement, you've also messed up my evening.' / A woman was shopping for a pair of shoes but couldn't get a fit, even though the shop assistant had one. / 'I'd like to kick him in the teeth, but why should I improve his looks?' / 'Your sister's spoiled, isn't she?' 'No, it's just the perfume she's wearing.' / What did Little John say when Robin Hood fired at him? That was an arrow escape. / What did the health attendant say to his girl assistant? Hi, Jean. / What sort of children does a florist have? Either budding geniuses, or blooming idiots. / Owing to a strike at the Meteorological Office there will be no weather tomorrow . . . / If you cross a ball of wool with a cat, do you get mittens? / 'My grandma has a wooden leg.' 'So what? My grandad's got an oak chest.' / What colour is a clear sky over Japan? Brew. / Sign in a cannibal's hut: I NEVER MET A MAN I DIDN'T LIKE. / What goes up in the air white and comes down yellow and white? An egg. / My mum's a business woman. She knows everybody's business. / How do you spell mousetrap in three letters? C-A-T. / What has four wheels and flies? A dust cart. / Did you hear about the man who is so dumb that his dog is teaching him how to throw a stick? / Did you hear about the tortoise salesman whose business was slow? / Sign in a watch repair shop: Please be patient, I only have two hands. / Lawyer: I wish I could have done more for you. Prisoner: No thanks, ten years is plenty. / 'I hate to tell you this, but your wife just fell in the wishing well.' 'It works!' / What kind of motorbike can cook eggs? A scrambler. / What do you call pigs who live together? Pen friends. / What did Vikings use for secret messages? The Norse code. / What is the cheapest way to get to Australia? Be born there. / Why did the sheep say moo? She was learning a foreign language. / Why didn't the piglets listen to their father? Because he was a boar. / 'One hundred tonnes of human hair was

JOKESJOKESJOKESJOKESJO

JOKES JOKES JOKES JOKES

stolen last night from a wig factory in Bridlington. Police are combing the area...' / What did the dying pup say? Well, I be doggone. / What is the difference between a gossip and an umbrella? You can shut up an umbrella. / What is the best system of book-keeping? Never lend them. / What man claps at Christmas? Santaplause. / Why is it difficult to keep a secret at the North Pole? Because your teeth chatter. / What is the difference between teachers and polos? People like polos. / What do geese watch on television? Duckumentaries. / How do you spell fool with one letter? When it's U. / Is it bad to write on an empty stomach? No, but it's better to write on paper. / A mad professor has just invented a new kind of teabag. It's waterproof. / What did the python say to its victim? 'I've got a crush on you.' / If a man smashed a clock, could he be accused of killing time? Not if the clock struck first. / What sort of lighting did Noah put in his ark? Flood lighting. / Did you hear about the girl who thought a potting shed was an indoor rifle range? / 'My auntie has a sore throat.' 'Well, buy her some Aunti-septic.' / Why did they put the acrobat in a sanitarium? Because he flipped out. / I was walking down the street the other day, and a motorist swerved off the road and knocked me down to avoid hitting a dog. / I got hiccups the other day and my teacher told me I could cure them by holding my breath and counting to one million. / What is everybody in the world doing at this very moment? Growing older. / Three boys were sharing a bed, but it was so crowded that one of them decided to sleep on the floor. After a while one of his friends told him to get back in bed. 'There's lots more room now,' he said. / Mary had a parrot, she killed it in a rage, for every time her boyfriend came the parrot told her age. / How do people eat cheese in Wales? Caerphilly. / What is curvy, yellow, and hangs about? A drip-dry banana. / How do you top a car? Tep on the brake, Tupid. / Dad: How did that window get broken? Boy: I was cleaning my catapult and it went off. / What fur did Adam and Eve wear? Bearskins. / Why did the fly fly? Because the spider spied her. / 'It looks like rain.' 'I know, but it says *Chicken Soup* on the packet.' / Why are dogs like trees? They both have barks. / Who can shave three times a day and still have a beard? A barber. / What did one casket say to the other casket? 'Is that you coffin?' / Nelly: Mummy, Jimmy just broke my doll. Mother: The naughty boy, how did that happen? Nelly: I hit him over the head with it. / 'Listen, when I want your opinion I'll give it to you.' / How do you pronounce VOLIX? Volume nine. / 'Does your dog have fleas?' 'Not that I know of. If he has he's too lazy to scratch them.' / Never believe a weather forecast of sunshine when the weatherman is wearing a raincoat. / What do you get if you cross a cow with a mule? Milk that has a real kick in it. / Who solved the murder of the Red Bean? Celery Queen. / What is the difference between television and a newspaper? You can't wrap fish and chips in a television. / 'Do you know gymnastics?' 'Jim who?' / Did you hear about the crook who was let out of prison but went behind bars? He bought his own pub. / What do you do if a sunbather collapses on the beach? Turn him over to get an even tan. /

JOKES JOKES JOKES JOKES

DRESSING UP/MAKING UP

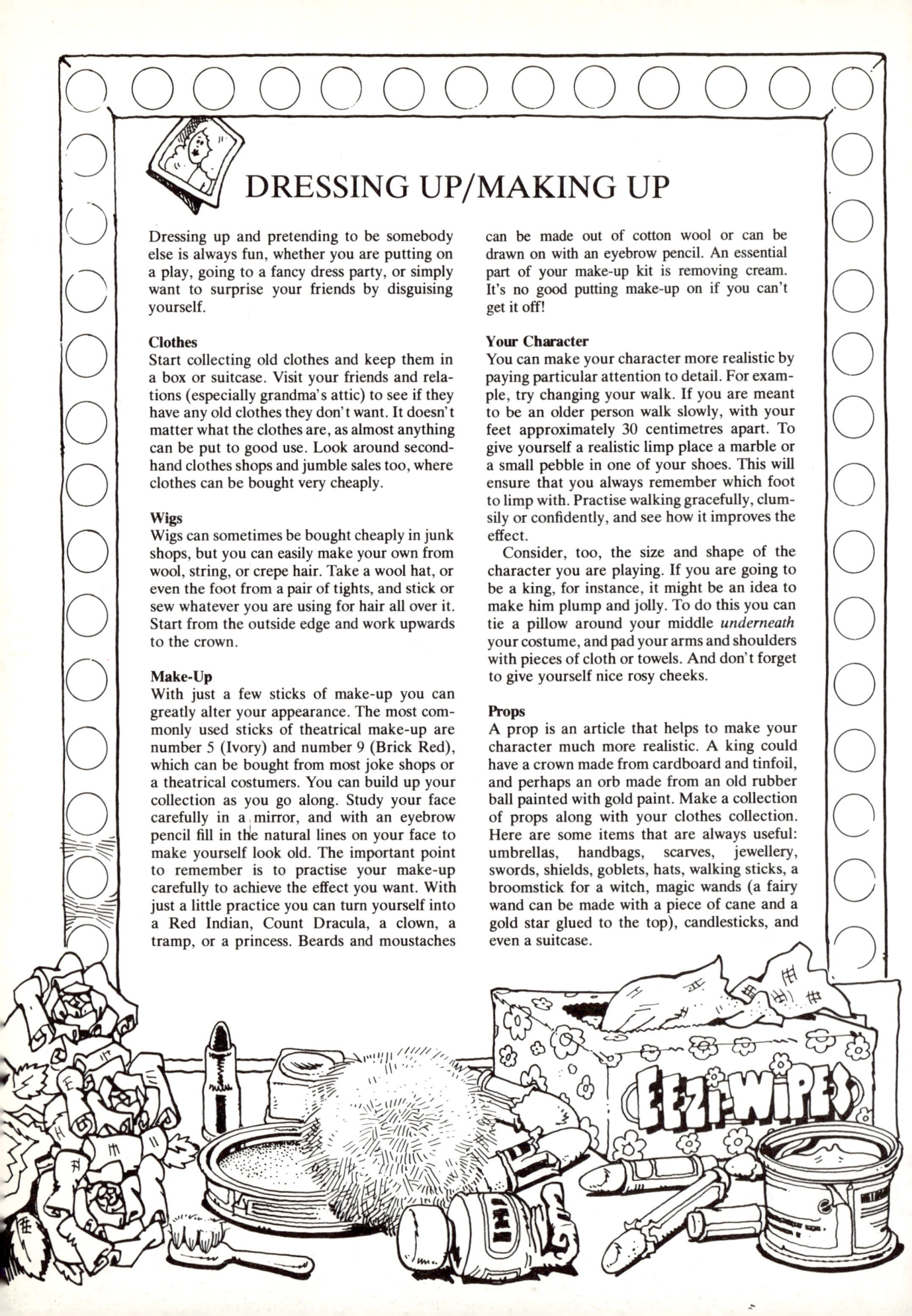

Dressing up and pretending to be somebody else is always fun, whether you are putting on a play, going to a fancy dress party, or simply want to surprise your friends by disguising yourself.

Clothes
Start collecting old clothes and keep them in a box or suitcase. Visit your friends and relations (especially grandma's attic) to see if they have any old clothes they don't want. It doesn't matter what the clothes are, as almost anything can be put to good use. Look around second-hand clothes shops and jumble sales too, where clothes can be bought very cheaply.

Wigs
Wigs can sometimes be bought cheaply in junk shops, but you can easily make your own from wool, string, or crepe hair. Take a wool hat, or even the foot from a pair of tights, and stick or sew whatever you are using for hair all over it. Start from the outside edge and work upwards to the crown.

Make-Up
With just a few sticks of make-up you can greatly alter your appearance. The most commonly used sticks of theatrical make-up are number 5 (Ivory) and number 9 (Brick Red), which can be bought from most joke shops or a theatrical costumers. You can build up your collection as you go along. Study your face carefully in a mirror, and with an eyebrow pencil fill in the natural lines on your face to make yourself look old. The important point to remember is to practise your make-up carefully to achieve the effect you want. With just a little practice you can turn yourself into a Red Indian, Count Dracula, a clown, a tramp, or a princess. Beards and moustaches can be made out of cotton wool or can be drawn on with an eyebrow pencil. An essential part of your make-up kit is removing cream. It's no good putting make-up on if you can't get it off!

Your Character
You can make your character more realistic by paying particular attention to detail. For example, try changing your walk. If you are meant to be an older person walk slowly, with your feet approximately 30 centimetres apart. To give yourself a realistic limp place a marble or a small pebble in one of your shoes. This will ensure that you always remember which foot to limp with. Practise walking gracefully, clumsily or confidently, and see how it improves the effect.

Consider, too, the size and shape of the character you are playing. If you are going to be a king, for instance, it might be an idea to make him plump and jolly. To do this you can tie a pillow around your middle *underneath* your costume, and pad your arms and shoulders with pieces of cloth or towels. And don't forget to give yourself nice rosy cheeks.

Props
A prop is an article that helps to make your character much more realistic. A king could have a crown made from cardboard and tinfoil, and perhaps an orb made from an old rubber ball painted with gold paint. Make a collection of props along with your clothes collection. Here are some items that are always useful: umbrellas, handbags, scarves, jewellery, swords, shields, goblets, hats, walking sticks, a broomstick for a witch, magic wands (a fairy wand can be made with a piece of cane and a gold star glued to the top), candlesticks, and even a suitcase.

The Madcap Giant Book of Jokes

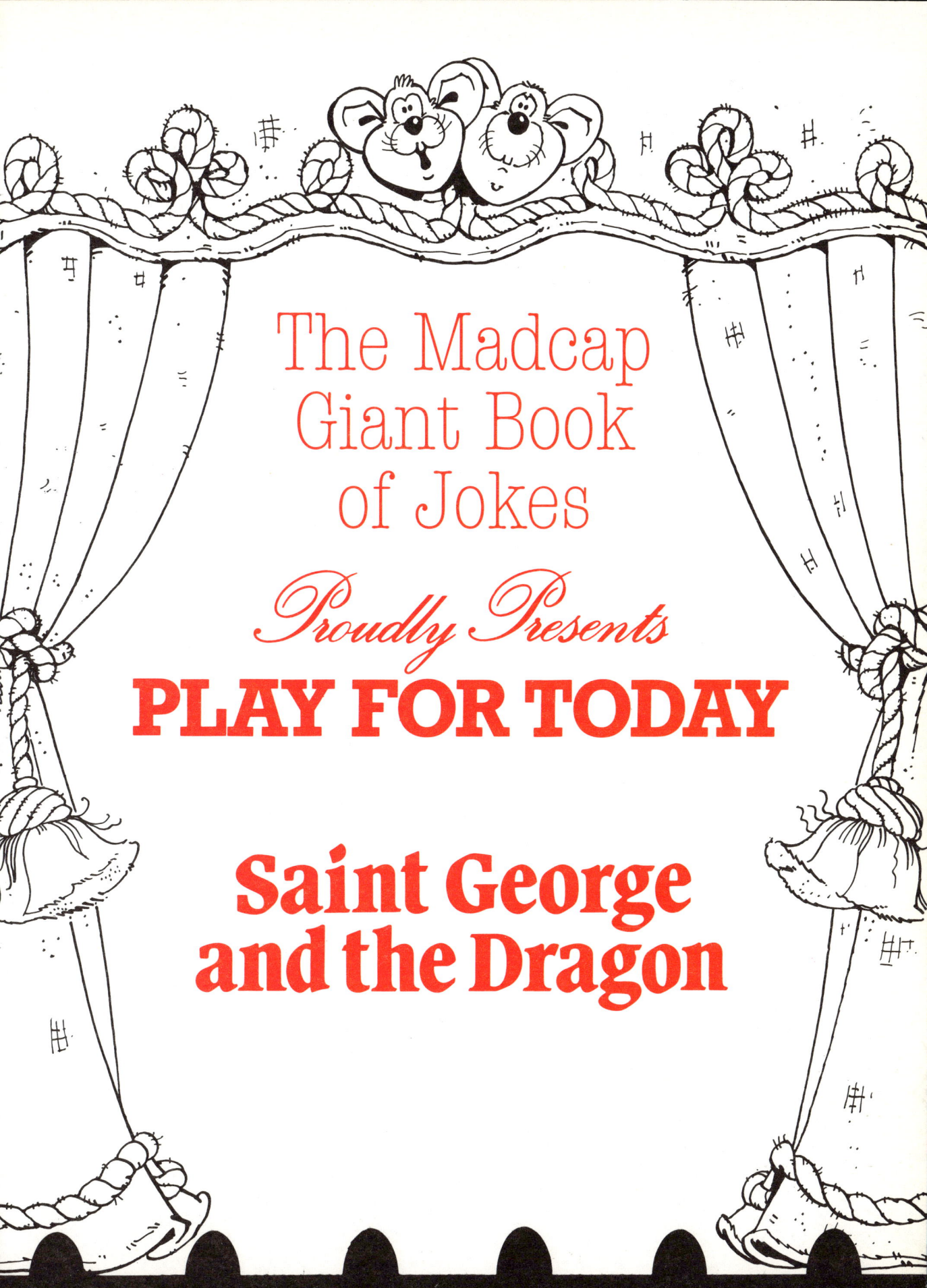

Proudly Presents

PLAY FOR TODAY

Saint George and the Dragon

SAINT GEORGE AND THE DRAGON

Here is a play that you can perform at any time of the year, and use as many actors as you have. If you only have a few you can roll the three Knights of the Triangular Table into one, or if you have lots of friends who wish to take part you can add more court lords and ladies and even put in an extra scene about the dragon fight between Acts One and Two.

The scenery is simple. All you need is a large throne for the king (an armchair will do well) and two smaller thrones for the Queen and Princess Poppet (kitchen chairs will do). The Knights and the Court Jester all sit on the floor. The costumes can be as grand or as simple as your wardrobe allows, but try to make the characters look as realistic as possible.

At all times speak loudly and be sure your audience can see as well as hear. Remember Sir Noel Coward's advice to a young actor: 'Speak clearly, and don't bump into the furniture!'

Characters:

KING KLONG, ruler of the Kingdom of Klipklop
QUEEN KLEAN, his wife
PRINCESS POPPET, their daughter
POFACE, the Court Jester
SIR LANCELOT
SIR LAUGHALOT   } Knights of the Triangular
SIR WINALOT   }   Table
SAINT GEORGE

ACT ONE: THE PALACE OF KING KLONG IN THE KINGDOM OF KLIPKLOP.

KING KLONG is seated on his throne, with his wife, QUEEN KLEAN, sitting on his right, and their daughter, PRINCESS POPPET, sitting on his left. POFACE, the Court Jester, is sitting at the feet of the king.

POFACE:	Come along, your majesty, this one will make you laugh.
KING KLONG:	I doubt it, Poface, I doubt it.
POFACE:	You just wait and see. Tell me, your majesty, what did the carpet say to the table?
KING KLONG:	I don't know, what *did* the carpet say to the table?
POFACE:	I can see your drawers!
KING KLONG:	That's very funny! Tell me another.
POFACE:	What did the picture say to the wall?
KING KLONG:	Well?
POFACE:	I've been framed!
KING KLONG:	Ho, ho, ho! That's very funny, very funny indeed.
QUEEN KLEAN:	Really, Klong, I don't see how you can laugh at a time like this.
KING KLONG:	You're quite right, my dear, but you know how I love a good riddle.
POFACE:	How about this one, your majesty? Why did the chicken . . .
KING KLONG:	No, Poface, no more. The Queen is quite right. This is no time for jesting. We've got work to do.
QUEEN KLEAN:	And it's no ordinary work, Klong. We've got to think of a way of saving dear Poppet's life.
PRINCESS POPPET:	There's nothing to be done, mother. I know that.
QUEEN KLEAN:	Don't be silly child. We're not going to give you up to that dreadful dragon without a fight – are we, Klong?
KING KLONG:	No, indeed, my dear. We'll save our little Princess Poppet, never fear.
PRINCESS POPPET:	But how, father?
KING KLONG:	{ Your mother will think of something!
QUEEN KLEAN:	{ Your father will think of something!
PRINCESS POPPET:	But we haven't much time. The dreadful dragon has to have one sixteen-year-old girl for his lunch every day and it's my turn today and that's all there is to it.
QUEEN KLEAN:	Couldn't we send him one of the kitchen maids? They're plumper than our Poppet. He'd find them much more tasty.
KING KLONG:	We haven't any sixteen-year-old kitchen maids left! He had the last one for high tea on Sunday.
QUEEN KLEAN:	You're right, so he did. What about the housekeeper?
KING KLONG:	But she's sixty!
QUEEN KLEAN:	He's so greedy, he'd never notice.
PRINCESS POPPET:	No, it wouldn't be fair. It's my turn and I must go. We told the people that every family would take it in turn and we must keep our word. Don't you agree?
KING KLONG:	I suppose so, my dear.
QUEEN KLEAN:	What would happen, do you think, if we just ignored him?
KING KLONG:	What do you mean, ignored him?
QUEEN KLEAN:	Well, didn't send him anyone for his lunch today.
KING KLONG:	He'd do what he said he would. He'd kill everyone in the kingdom.
QUEEN KLEAN:	Oh, dear!
KING KLONG:	Yes, dear?
QUEEN KLEAN:	What *are* we going to do?

PRINCESS POPPET:	It's half-past ten. I'd better go and clean my teeth and pack my bag.
KING KLONG:	What are you going to pack?
PRINCESS POPPET:	My overnight things, I thought.
KING KLONG:	Oh, I don't think you'll be needing those.
PRINCESS POPPET:	Perhaps I could take the dreadful dragon a present of some sort, as a kind of peace offering.
KING KLONG:	You mean, something like a napkin ring and a bottle of ketchup?
QUEEN KLEAN:	Oh, dear!
KING KLONG:	Yes, de . . .
QUEEN KLEAN:	KLONG! I want you to do something and I want you to do that something NOW!
KING KLONG:	Yes, dear. What dear?
QUEEN KLEAN:	I don't know, you royal dunderhead. That's why I want *you* to do it. If I knew what to do I'd be doing it myself!
KING KLONG:	I know. Perhaps I could give my cousin King Arthur a ring. He always has lots of good ideas.
QUEEN KLEAN:	That's a right royal idea. You're not as much a fool as you look.
POFACE:	I'm afraid you can't do that, your majesty.
KING KLONG:	What do you mean, Poface?
QUEEN KLEAN:	What on earth are you jabbering about, Poface? Kings and Queens are at work, you worm! This is no time for idle jests! Klong, off you go immediately and call Arthur.
POFACE:	But you can't, your majesty!
KING KLONG:	And why not?
POFACE:	Because the telephone hasn't been invented yet.
KING KLONG:	Are you sure?
POFACE:	Quite sure. The telephone is going to be invented in about one thousand years' time by Alexander Graham Bellowski, the original telegraph Pole. That's a joke.
QUEEN KLEAN:	Oh, dear.
KING KLONG:	Yes, dear. I mean, sorry, dear. What about the Post Office – has that been invented yet?
POFACE:	I'm afraid not. But that reminds me of a riddle.
QUEEN KLEAN:	Oh no!
KING KLONG:	Oh yes!
POFACE:	How do you make a Maltese Cross?
KING KLONG:	Stamp on his foot!
POFACE:	Correct! And what do you call a rabbit that sits down on the stove by mistake?
KING KLONG:	A little hot cross bun!
QUEEN KLEAN:	Oh, dear.
KING KLONG:	Yes, de . . . ! Whoops! I didn't say a thing.
PRINCESS POPPET:	Don't worry. I know there's nothing to be done.
QUEEN KLEAN:	There must be something. Poface, we need your help. Who can save us? Aren't there any dragon tamers in Klipklop?
POFACE:	I'm afraid not, your majesty.
QUEEN KLEAN:	No truly brave and valiant warriors?
POFACE:	Not really, unless you count the Knights of the Triangular Table.
KING KLONG:	Of course, of course, the Knights of the Triangular Table! Well done, Poface! Our troubles are ended. The terrible trio will save us now.
PRINCESS POPPET:	Do you think so, father?
KING KLONG:	Think so? I KNOW so, Poppet! Go and get 'em, Poface. Where are they?
POFACE:	Playing Ludo in the antechamber.
KING KLONG:	Are they alone?
POFACE:	No, they've got a knight from a neighbouring kingdom with them. He's on a fact-finding tour of Klipklop.
KING KLONG:	Well, bring them in, man, bring them in.

(POFACE *goes to the door, flings it open, and calls*)

POFACE:	His Most Excellent, Gracious and Royal Majesty King Klong of Klipklop requests and requires the immediate pleasure of the company of his three knights of the Triangular Table together with their Ludo partner, the friendly knight from the neighbouring kingdom!

(POFACE *returns to his place at the feet of* KING KLONG *and the four knights –* SIR LANCELOT, SIR LAUGHALOT, SIR WINALOT *and* SAINT GEORGE *– make their entrance. They stand in a line in front of the throne.*)

KING KLONG:	Welcome, gentlemen, welcome. What lovely weather we're having. Have you heard the one about the farmer who took his cow to the vet because she was so moooo-dy?!
QUEEN KLEAN:	Get to the point, Klong.
KING KLONG:	The point? Oh, yes, the point! Gentlemen, we need your help.
QUEEN KLEAN:	We need it desperately.
PRINCESS POPPET:	We need it urgently.
KING KLONG:	We need it now. Will you help us?
THE KNIGHTS:	Of course! To be sure! Without a doubt! You can count on us!
KING KLONG:	Good men. Now let me ask each of you something first. (*He points to* SIR WINALOT) Now, sir, what's your name?
SIR WINALOT:	Sir Winalot, your majesty.

KING KLONG:	That's a good name for a knight. Now tell me, are you a brave man?
SIR WINALOT:	I'm not only brave, sire. I am the bravest man in the whole kingdom of Klipklop.
KING KLONG:	I'm delighted to hear it. (*Points to SIR LAUGHALOT who steps forward*) Now, you sir, what is your name?
SIR LAUGHALOT:	Sir Laughalot, sire.
KING KLONG:	That's a cheerful name. It's better than mine, don't you think so, Klean, dear?
QUEEN KLEAN:	Stop chattering, Klong, and get on with it.
KING KLONG:	Of course, dear, of course. Now, Sir Laughalot, are *you* brave?
SIR LAUGHALOT:	Am I brave? I'm as brave as a lion, as quick as a tiger, as fierce as an ogre, as great as a storm. I'm as strong as an elephant. As mighty as mountains. Ferocious as volcanoes. I'm as sharp as lightning, as furious as thunder, I'm . . .
KING KLONG:	Thank you very much. I've got the idea. Now you. (*Points to SIR LANCELOT*) What's your name?
SIR LANCELOT:	Sir Dancealot, sire.
KING KLONG:	That's funny, I thought your name was Lancelot.
SIR LANCELOT:	That's right, your majesty, Sir Dancealot.
POFACE:	I think Sir Lancelot has a cold in the nose, your majesty.
SIR LANCELOT:	Dat's right. A cold in de ´dose, your majesty.
KING KLONG:	In that case, don't come too near. I don't want to catch it.
POFACE:	I knew an elephant who was a spy. He had a code in his trunk!
KING KLONG:	Now, Sir Dancealot, I mean, Sir Lancelot, are you brave?
SIR LANCELOT:	Me, sire? I'm de bravest man of de whole trio. Aitchoooo!
KING KLONG:	Bless you.
SIR LANCELOT:	Dank do.
KING KLONG:	You're welcome. Now, you sire. (*Points to SAINT GEORGE who steps forward and bows*) What lovely manners! And what's your name?
SAINT GEORGE:	George, your majesty.
KING KLONG:	Just George, eh? And brave, too?
SAINT GEORGE:	I hope so, your majesty.
KING KLONG:	You hope so? That's a bit feeble. You're not supposed to hope around here, you know. All my knights are *sure* about what I ask them. What do you think of him, dear? I mean, he's not even called *Sir* George, and he only *hopes* he's brave.
QUEEN KLEAN:	But as you said yourself, he's got lovely manners.
PRINCESS POPPET:	And I rather like him.
KING KLONG:	Keep quiet, Poppet, this has nothing to do with you.
PRINCESS POPPET:	But father . . .
QUEEN KLEAN:	Hush, child, your father's quite right for once.
KING KLONG:	Well, gentlemen, since you all seem to be more or less brave, I've got a teensy-weensy little favour to ask of you.
THE KNIGHTS:	Anything, your majesty.
KING KLONG:	Well, it's like this. Every day that dreadful dragon that lives on the hill has to have a succulent sixteen-year-old girl for his lunch, and today's the day when my dear daughter here is due to be the main dish at the dragon's feast. Now, we'd like you bold and brave knights to pop up the hill and pop off the dragon. What do you say to that?
SIR WINALOT: SIR LAUGHALOT: SIR LANCELOT:	AITCHOOOO!
KING KLONG:	Bless you!
SIR WINALOT: SIR LAUGHALOT: SIR LANCELOT:	Dank do.
KING KLONG:	You're welcome. Now, lads, what do you say to my plan?
SIR WINALOT:	Oh, fordive me, dour majesdy, but I seem to have caught Sir Dancelot's dold in de dose. I was out late at a Knightclub and I don't feel at all well.
KING KLONG:	Sir Laughalot?
SIR LAUGHALOT:	Me doo, dour majesdy. Wid did derrible cold in de dose I don't dink I'm up to killing the dragon.
KING KLONG:	And how do you feel now, Sir Lancelot?
SIR LANCELOT:	Dreadful, dour majesdy. Worse dan ever. I dot to lie down.
KING KLONG:	That seems to leave us with poor old George here. Will you go and kill the dragon for us?
SAINT GEORGE:	It will be an honour, sire.
EVERYONE:	What did he say?
THE LADIES: THE KNIGHTS:	He's a hero! The man's mad!
KING KLONG:	Look, George, old boy, are my eyes deceiving me or did I hear you say you'd go and kill our dreadful daughter and save the pretty dragon?
SAINT GEORGE:	I will go up the hill and, God willing, I will slay the dreadful dragon and save the beautiful Princess Poppet.
PRINCESS POPPET:	That's wonderful.
KING KLONG:	There's no time to lose, George. Here, take Poppet with you and do your best.
PRINCESS POPPET:	Goodbye, mother and father. Goodbye, Poface.
EVERYONE:	Goodbye, Poppet, and good luck George! (*All wave*)

ACT TWO: KING KLONG'S PALACE TWO HOURS LATER.

The KING and QUEEN are on their thrones, POFACE is at their feet. The KNIGHTS are trying to play tennis.

THE KNIGHTS:	Aitchoooo!
KING KLONG:	Bless you!
THE KNIGHTS:	Dank do.
KING KLONG:	You're welcome.
POFACE:	Why is being fat not very funny?
KING KLONG:	Because you can't laugh it off!
QUEEN KLEAN:	Oh, dear!
KING KLONG:	Yes, dear?
QUEEN KLEAN:	Where are they?
KING KLONG:	Over there playing tennis. They're being very noisy. I suppose it's because they're all raising a racquet!
QUEEN KLEAN:	I don't mean them, you royal nitwit! I mean Poppet and that Mr George.
KING KLONG:	With the dragon I suppose.
QUEEN KLEAN:	What are they doing all this time – taking tea?
KING KLONG:	No, dear. It's far too early in the afternoon.
QUEEN KLEAN:	Well, why aren't they back?

(The doors burst open and PRINCESS POPPET runs in followed by GEORGE)

PRINCESS POPPET:	We *are* back, mother!

(EVERYONE cheers)

QUEEN KLEAN:	I can hardly believe it! You're back—
PRINCESS POPPET:	And safe and sound!
KING KLONG:	And is the dragon dead?
PRINCESS POPPET:	As dead as a dodo!
POFACE:	I'm afraid dodos haven't been invented yet.
PRINCESS POPPET:	I saw the dragon killed with my own eyes. It's all thanks to George.
KING KLONG:	Of course, of course, George, old man, I was quite forgetting you. We'll bake a special pie to celebrate. What's the best thing to put in it?
POFACE:	Your teeth!
KING KLONG:	Don't be silly, Poface. And well done, George my boy.
SAINT GEORGE:	It was nothing.
PRINCESS POPPET:	Don't be silly, George. You were wonderfully brave. Father, you must give him a reward.
KING KLONG:	Of course I must, and I will. We are all so grateful to you, George, you can have anything you like, just name it and it's yours.
SAINT GEORGE:	There is only one thing you have to give that I would like, your majesty. I would like your daughter's hand in marriage.
KING KLONG:	My daughter's what in where?
SAINT GEORGE:	Your daughter's hand in marriage.
PRINCESS POPPET:	Oh, father, do say yes!
KING KLONG:	What do you think, dear?
QUEEN KLEAN:	I don't see why not. After all, he did save our daughter and he has got lovely manners.
KING KLONG:	But we don't even know his name. What comes before the George, that's what I want to know.
POFACE:	I think it's Saint, your majesty.
KING KLONG:	Saint George? Well, that sounds rather good. And you'd like to marry this Saint George chappie would you, Poppet?
PRINCESS POPPET:	I would, father, very very much.
KING KLONG:	And does everyone at court approve?
KNIGHTS:	We wholeheartedly approve, your majesty.
KING KLONG:	Your colds got better quickly, that's nice! Well, George, everyone agrees. You're a brave man, you've earned your reward and may marry Princess Poppet. What do you say to that?
SAINT GEORGE:	Aitchooo!
KING KLONG:	Bless you!
SAINT GEORGE:	Dank do.
KING KLONG:	You're welcome.

(Everyone laughs. SAINT GEORGE and PRINCESS POPPET join hands. Everyone cheers.)

THE END

IF YOU HAVE A QUESTION TO ASK DURING A TEST, RAISE YOUR RIGHT ARM.
THE BLOOD WILL DRAIN FROM YOUR ARM TO YOUR BRAIN, SO THAT YOU CAN SOLVE THE PROBLEM ON YOUR OWN.

WHAT HAPPENS TO STUDENTS WHO THINK THAT ELECTRICITY IS EASY?
THEY GET A SHOCK!

'WHAT IS USED AS A CONDUCTOR OF ELECTRICITY?'
— 'WHY... ER...'
'WIRE IS RIGHT!'

'DID YOU GET A GOOD PLACE IN YOUR EXAMS?'
'YES, NEXT TO THE RADIATOR!'

'Timmy, how can you prove that the world is round?'
'I never said it was, Miss!'

WHY WAS GOLIATH SURPRISED WHEN DAVID HIT HIM WITH A STONE?
— IT HAD NEVER ENTERED HIS HEAD BEFORE!

'WHAT IS THE UNIT OF ELECTRICAL POWER?'
'THE WHAT—?'
'CORRECT!'

WHAT EXAMS DO HORSES TAKE?
HAY LEVELS!

WHAT HAPPENED TO THE PLANT IN THE MATHS CLASS?
— IT GREW SQUARE ROOTS!

IF YOU LOST FOUR FINGERS IN AN ACCIDENT, WHAT WOULD YOU HAVE?
— NO MORE PIANO LESSONS!

DO YOU KNOW WHAT THE ZULUS DO WITH BANANA SKINS?
— THROW THEM AWAY, OF COURSE!

WHAT IS AN ABNORMAL STUDENT?
— ONE WHO REMEMBERS TO BRING HIS HOMEWORK BACK AFTER THE HOLIDAYS!

WHO WROTE: 'TO A FIELD MOUSE'?
— WHOEVER IT WAS, I BET HE DIDN'T GET A REPLY!

DID YOU HEAR ABOUT THE CROSS-EYED TEACHER?
— SHE COULDN'T CONTROL HER PUPILS!

IF I HAD FORTY APPLES IN ONE HAND, AND FIFTY IN THE OTHER, WHAT WOULD I HAVE? *Big hands*

NAME THREE COLLECTIVE NOUNS. *The dustpan, the rubbish bin, and the vacuum cleaner.*

WHICH MONTH HAS 28 DAYS? *They all have.*

WHERE DO INSECTS GO IN WINTER? *Search me!*

LATIN IS A DEAD LANGUAGE, AS DEAD AS IT CAN BE; IT KILLED OFF ALL THE ROMANS, AND NOW IT'S KILLING ME!

WHY DID THE SCHOOLBOY STAND ON HIS HEAD? — HE WAS TURNING THINGS OVER IN HIS HEAD!

WHY DID THE TEACHER MARRY THE CARETAKER? BECAUSE HE SWEPT HER OFF HER FEET!

What is the most Popular Phrase at school? — I DON'T KNOW!

REPORT
ISABEL POTTS IS A GOOD PUPIL! BUT SHE TALKS TOO MUCH.
You should meet her mother!
signed: Mr. Potts

WHAT'S THE DIFFERENCE BETWEEN A SCHOOL TEACHER AND A TRAIN? — A TEACHER SAYS: 'SPIT THE TOFFEE OUT!' A TRAIN SAYS: 'CHEW CHEW'

What is the difference between a lemon and a white elephant?
The lemon is yellow.

What is the difference between an elephant and a biscuit?
You can't dip an elephant in your tea.

Why do elephants have wrinkled ankles?
They lace their shoes too tightly.

Why does an elephant have cracks between his toes?
To hold his bus ticket.

What do you give an exhausted elephant?
Trunkquillizers.

Why did the elephant paint her head yellow?
To see if blondes had more fun.

What do you get when you cross a whale with an elephant?
Very big swimming trunks.

Sign in an elephant factory: THINK BIG!

Elephant Trainer: My elephant has just swallowed a camera.
Vet: Don't worry, sir, nothing will develop.

With what words do you scold an elephant?
Tusk, tusk!

EDNA: Have a peanut.
ALMA: No thanks, they're fattening.
EDNA: Fattening?
ALMA: Yes. Ever seen a skinny elephant?

How do you get an elephant in a matchbox?
Take the matches out first.

SAMMY: What's the difference between an elephant and upduck.
TAMMY: What's upduck?
SAMMY: Nothing much, dearie.

Why don't you go into the jungle after six o'clock?
Because of elephants falling out of trees.

Why did the elephant tie a knot in his trunk?
So that he wouldn't forget.

What is the difference between a flea and an elephant?
An elephant can have fleas, but a flea can't have elephants.

60

Do you know why giraffes are nosey?
Because they're always looking over the wall to
 see what giraffe-ter (you're after).

Is a baby giraffe ever taller than its mother?
Yes, when it sits on its father's shoulders.

What do you call a giraffe that stands on your toe?
Anything you like; its head is too far away to hear
 you.

What do you get if you cross a giraffe with a dog?
An animal that barks at low flying aircraft.

Does the giraffe get a sore throat if he gets wet
 feet?
Yes, but not until next week.

For what other reason does a giraffe have a long
 neck?
Because its feet smell.

What is a giraffe's favourite joke?
A tall story.

Why do giraffes have long necks?
To connect their heads to their bodies.

Why do giraffes have such a small appetite?
Because a little goes a long way.

What is worse than a giraffe with a sore throat?
A giraffe with a stiff neck.

DOTTY DOODLES

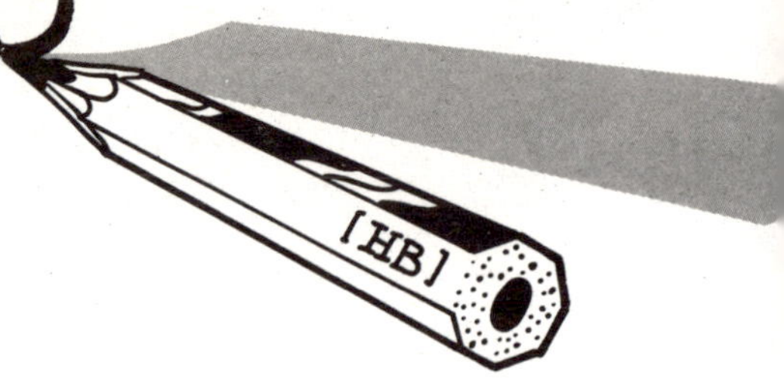

Dotty doodles is a game that can be played anywhere, anytime, whether you are on a train or a plane, or snowbound at the North Pole. You only need a piece of paper and a pencil, or failing that you can use your finger in the snow or sand!

Here's what to do:

1. Draw a doodle:

2. Get your friend to turn it into a picture *and* give it a title:

KNAVE OF HEARTS

Here are some doodles for you to turn into pictures:

1.

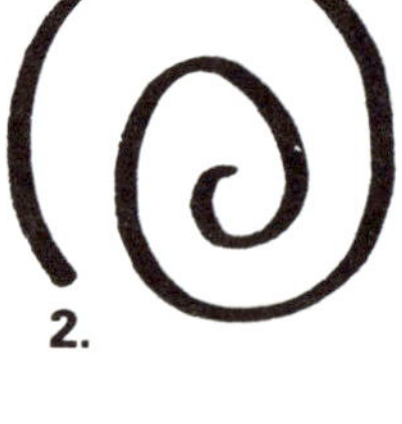

2.

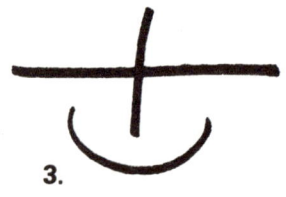

3.

4.

5.

I CAN'T DRAW!

Try these tricky tonguetwisters twenty times:

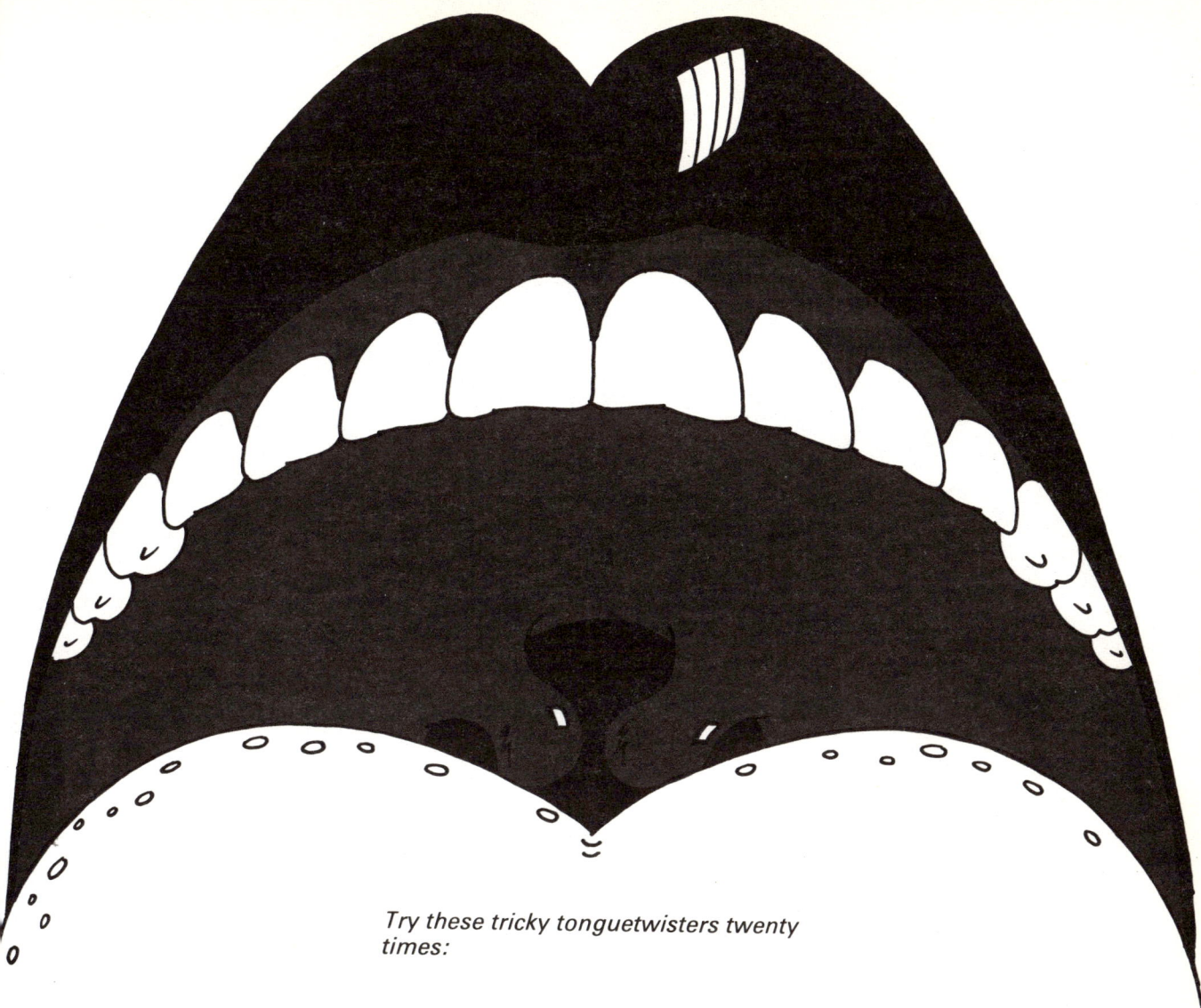

If Harry hurries, will hairy Henry hand him a hundred hammers?

Six skyscrapers stood side by side, shimmering by the seashore.

Ninety-nine naughty knitted nick-nacks were nicked by ninety-nine naughty knitted nick-nack nickers.

Sammy Smilie smelt a smell of small-coal
Did Sammy Smilie smell a smell of small-coal?
If Sammy Smilie smelt a smell of small-coal,
Where's the smell of small-coal Sammy Smilie smelt?

Esther Elephant eats eighty-eight Easter eggs eagerly every Easter.

She sells sea-shells on the sea-shore.

Pitter-patter pitter-patter, rather than patter-pitter patter pitter.

Our black bull bled black blood on our blackthorn flower.

Quixote Quicksight quizzed a queerish quidbox.
Did Quixote Quicksight quiz a queerish quidbox?
If Quixote Quicksight quizzed a queerish quidbox,
Where's the queerish quidbox Quixote Quicksight quizzed?

Slim Sam shaved six slippery chins in sixty-six seconds.

Am I and Amy aiming anaemic anemones on my many enemies?

Meek Morgan Matthews made weak Matty Morgan many milkshakes.

'Hark, an aardvark!' Mark barked for a lark.

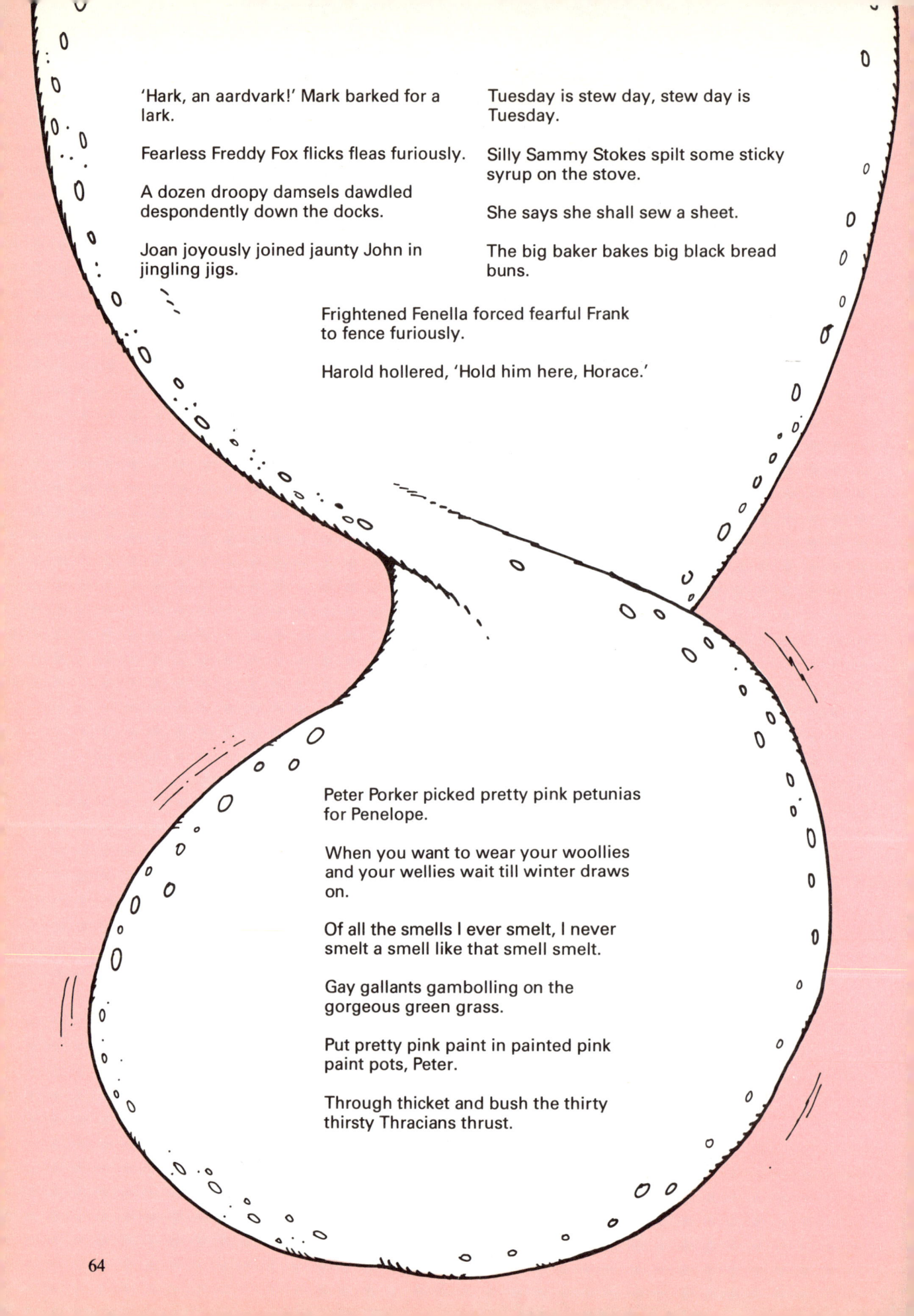

Fearless Freddy Fox flicks fleas furiously.

A dozen droopy damsels dawdled despondently down the docks.

Joan joyously joined jaunty John in jingling jigs.

Frightened Fenella forced fearful Frank to fence furiously.

Harold hollered, 'Hold him here, Horace.'

Tuesday is stew day, stew day is Tuesday.

Silly Sammy Stokes spilt some sticky syrup on the stove.

She says she shall sew a sheet.

The big baker bakes big black bread buns.

Peter Porker picked pretty pink petunias for Penelope.

When you want to wear your woollies and your wellies wait till winter draws on.

Of all the smells I ever smelt, I never smelt a smell like that smell smelt.

Gay gallants gambolling on the gorgeous green grass.

Put pretty pink paint in painted pink paint pots, Peter.

Through thicket and bush the thirty thirsty Thracians thrust.

EMERGENCY JOKES

There are times in anyone's life when things go wrong:

........You break the family teapot.

........You miss the school bus.

........You get ice skates for Christmas and it doesn't snow.

........You get ill on a Friday night.

........Your parents move home while you're at school.

........The wind stops blowing when you get your kite out.

........Your television breaks down in the middle of your favourite programme.

........Your homework blows away on the way to school.

........Your Midsummer's Eve party is snowed out.

........It rains on Guy Fawkes night.

........Rain stops play when it's your turn to bat.

........You get infected with poison ivy bending over to pick a four-leaf clover.

........You borrow your friend's football boots and the dog chews them.

........Lightning strikes your new aluminium tennis racquet.

........Your favourite pop group visit your town while you are on holiday.

........You know the answer to all the questions in the test, *except* the one the teacher asks you.

IN THE EVENT OF EMERGENCY turn the page

........A tornado carries off your new bike.

........It rains heavily *after* your house burns down.

... tell a joke! It'll cheer you up and make everyone forget their worries. Here are some jokes to tell:

Why did the poor dog chase his tail?
To make both ends meet.

What do you call mad fleas?
Loony ticks.

Why couldn't the boy sleep in class?
Because the teacher talked too loudly.

CUSTOMER: These safety matches you sold me won't light.
SHOPKEEPER: Well, you can't get much safer than that!

DOCTOR: Diet!
PATIENT: What colour?

Where did Napoleon keep his armies?
Up his sleevies.

What kind of seagull can't fly?
A bi-seagull (bicycle).

Shall I tell you the joke about the pencil?
No, there's no point in it!

'I'm not myself tonight.'
'I noticed the improvement.'

A taxi driver slowed down by the kerb, wound down the window and called to a passer-by, 'Oi! Leatherhead?' To which the passer-by replied: 'Fishface!'

'Monica, if I bought 50 loaves of bread for £1·00, what would each one be?'
'Stale, miss.'

'What's a Grecian urn?'
'About fifty quid a week, I should think.'

'Gerald's taking a sandwich course.'
'Why?'
'To earn his bread and butter.'

BOY: Can I carry your bag, sir?
MAN: No, let her walk.

EXCUSE ME, IS THIS A BARKING BUS?

NO MADAM, IT ONLY GOES 'HONK-HONK'.

PUPIL: How can I improve my piano playing?
MUSIC MASTER: Try playing with the lid down.

BIG SISTER: I wish I had a penny for every boy who wanted to marry me.
LITTLE BROTHER: What would you do, buy a packet of polos?

Plymouth Argyle lost all their matches so the manager brought along a demon for luck. They won against Arsenal 52–0 and won against Spurs 36–0. When the players asked why, the manager replied: 'Demons are Argyle's best friend.'

What is the definition of an archaeologist?
A man whose career is in ruins.

MOTHER: Anita, there were two chocolate cakes in the larder and now there's only one. Why?
ANITA: It must have been so dark I didn't see the other one.

Why did the Manager of a blotting paper company not want to retire?
He found the job too absorbing.

The Pleasure of your Company is Requested at the Mad Hatter's Tea Party

What to wear at a Mad Hatter's Tea Party
The most important thing to wear at a Mad Hatter's Tea Party is, of course, a funny hat. Here is how to make one:

Top Hat
1. A top hat can be made out of cardboard. Take a piece that will fit around your head and make it into a tube:

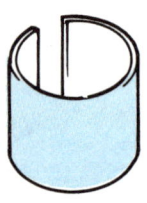

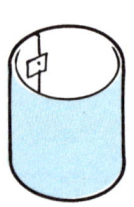

2. To make the brim cut out a large circle by drawing around a very large dinner plate. Cut a hole in the centre big enough to get your head through, like this:

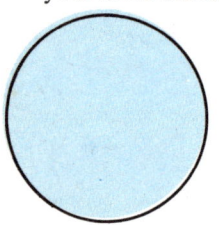

3. Push the triangles up and glue to the inside of your tube:

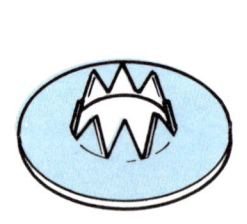

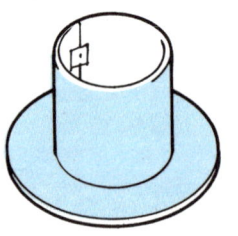

4. A circle can be sellotaped on the top of the hat. Paint it black and you have a top hat!

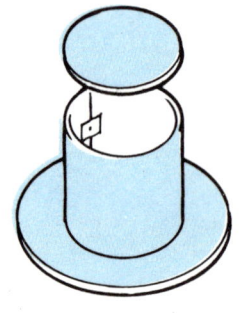

DO YOU KNOW THE STORY OF THE EMPTY TEA-CUP?
NO.
THERE'S NOTHING IN IT!
IT LOOKS LIKE RAIN!
WELL, THERE'S SIX TEABAGS IN THE POT!
MY FRIEND FELL FROM A WINDOW TWENTY STOREYS UP YESTERDAY–
WAS HE HURT?
NO, HE FELL INSIDE!
I SAY, YOU'VE GOT YOUR HAT ON BACK TO FRONT!
HOW DO YOU KNOW WHICH WAY I'M GOING?
DO NOT DISTURB
I BET I KNOW WHERE YOU'RE GOING TONIGHT!
WHERE?
TO SLEEP!
WHAT BEGINS WITH T, ENDS WITH T AND HAS T IN THE MIDDLE?
I DON'T KNOW– WHAT?
A TEAPOT!
THIS BUN TASTES JUST LIKE SOAP!
THAT'S BECAUSE IT'S A BATH BUN!

FOR SALE & WA[NT]

Wanted: Mattress by gentleman stuffed with horsehair.

FOR SALE: To a good owner, fully grown and domesticated leopard. Able to roam free and untied, will eat flesh from the hand. Offers please.

FOR SALE: Hepplewhite table, property of titled lady with exquisitely carved legs.

Deep freeze: Scotch beef from Wales.

Room wanted for gentleman with good view and gas stove.

Piano: Would suit a beginner with chipped legs.

FOR SALE: Hammers, would suit any handyman, with claw head.

Delightful country cottage, 2 bedrooms, large lounge, kitchen, bathroom, coloured suite, toilet 5 miles from Epsom.

AMAZING OFFER. Fish and chip fryer, made from chip-[resist]ant enamel.

Please note: Rings can be ordered by post. Simply state size required or enclose strin[g] tied around your finger.

UNEMPLOYED man se[eks] work. Completely honest [and] trustworthy, will take [any]thing.

Bulldog for sale. Wha[t is] offered for ths one-[year] dog? Will eat anythin[g,] especially fond of chi[ldren.]

Widows made to o[rder,] us your specificatio[ns.]

A young lady w[anted for] and cleaning t[hree times a] week.

WANTED [–] cooker suitab[le] with white e[namel]

LOST an [oil painting] depicting [George] Bush on S[…]

FOR SA[LE …] lain [...] Belong[ed to …] crack[ed …]

BIC[YCLE for] sale [...] bo[...]
brooch

1929 Rolls-Royce hearse for sale – original body.

FOR SALE genuine synthetic wigs. Real 100% man-made fibre, perfectly natural. Looks just like real hair. Colours red, green, mauve, orange and blue.

LADY required for 6 hours work per week to clean small officers.

BED AND BREAKFAST, reasonable rates, comfortable beds, hot and cold running water in every room.

Chelmsford Conservative Club annual cheese and wind party to be held next Sunday evening.

HELP WANTED: Man to handle dynamite. Must be prepared to travel unexpectedly.

FOR SALE: Doctor's caravan and trailer. Doctor no further use.

FOR SALE beautiful wedding dress. Only worn twice.

Intelligent young lady required. Must speak proper and have good speling.

CRASH COURSES available

SHAGGY DOG STORIES

Lucy's mother had invented Mr and Mrs Snodgrass to dinner. They arrived early, and Lucy's father and mother were busy in the kitchen, so Lucy went into the living room to entertain the guests.

Mrs Snodgrass said to her husband, 'She isn't very p-r-e-t-t-y, is she?' spelling out the word.

'Perhaps not,' answered Lucy, 'but she is very b-r-i-g-h-t.'

The Englishman sat calmly in his garden and watched a flying saucer land. The creature that emerged had three eyes – one orange, one yellow, one green – and fangs. It walked on its elbows, and its nose lit up like a light bulb. 'Take me to your leader!' it commanded. 'Nonsense,' said the Englishman, stirring his tea, 'what you need is a plastic surgeon.'

A young man left university and got his first job as a door-to-door salesman, selling encyclopaedias. He went from house to house all day without making one single sale. Very depressed, he went to the last house on his list and a woman opened the door. The young man, in a burst of enthusiasm, gave his sales talk about the encyclopaedias: '. . . they are a mine of information, with all you need to know on cookery, gardening, history, politics, insurance, physics, chemistry, geography, and even psychology. There are twelve leather-bound volumes, each with 1,500 pages, which makes it three inches thick . . .'

'Hang on a moment,' said the woman and went inside and closed the door. After a few minutes she returned and said:

'I'll take volumes one and two.'

'Why only one and two,' asked the puzzled salesman, 'why not all twelve volumes?'

'Because,' said the woman, 'the broken leg of our table is only six inches short.'

At one house, when the dustman called round to empty the bins, the occupier had overslept and forgotten to put his bin out. The dustman rang the bell and tapped on the door. After ten minutes, an upstairs window opened and a sleepy head looked out.

'Where's yer bin?' asked the dustman.

'I bin asleep,' came the reply, 'where's you bin?'

There was once a boy who found an Aladdin's lamp. He rubbed the lamp and out came a genie.

'I grant you three wishes,' said the genie.

'My first wish,' said the boy, 'is for a glass and a bottle of ginger beer, and when you pour it out, the bottle fills up again.'

'Your wish has been granted,' said the genie, and the boy received an empty glass and a bottle of ginger beer. He poured himself a glass full of ginger beer and immediately the bottle refilled itself. He drank the ginger beer and poured another glass. Once more the bottle magically filled again.

'It works!' said the boy, delighted. 'I'll have two more bottles please.'

Anybody can capture a crocodile. This is how to go about it. First get a telescope, a matchbox, a pair of tweezers, and a large, very boring book. Then choose a steamy hot day and go to the riverbank where crocodiles live. Just sit down, with the telescope, matchbox, and tweezers next to you and start to read. Since the day is warm and the book is dull, you will soon fall asleep.

A crocodile will see you after a while and naturally will come to investigate. He will peer over your shoulder at the book and start to read it. Because the day is hot and the book is dull, he too will fall asleep.

As soon as he does, you wake up. Pick up the telescope and look at the crocodile through the wrong end. Then, using the tweezers, pick him up and put him into the matchbox. And there you have your crocodile.

Some cowboys were sitting around a campfire telling stories. One of them said, 'I know an Indian who never forgets anything. The Devil can have my soul if I'm not telling the truth.'

That night the Devil appeared and said, 'Come along with me.'

'I was telling the truth,' the cowboy replied. 'I'll show you.'

The two of them went to the Indian. 'Do you like eggs?' the Devil asked.

'Yes,' the Indian replied.

Then the cowboy and the Devil went away. Twenty years later, the Devil heard that the cowboy had died, and he went off to find the Indian.

'How!' the Devil said, greeting him Indian-style with his right arm raised.

'Fried,' the Indian answered.

There were once three squaws. One sat on a leopard skin. One sat on a doe skin. The third sat on a hippopotamus skin. The squaw on the leopard skin had one son. The squaw on the deer skin had one son. But the squaw on the hippopotamus skin had twin sons. This all goes to prove that the squaw on the hippopotamus is equal to the sons of the squaws on the other two hides.

A pilot in the airforce was given the prototype of a new plane to test. It was supposed to be able to go at 2,000 kilometres an hour. He took off and climbed higher and higher, getting faster and faster. He crashed through the sound barrier with one almighty bang and continued up into the heavens. He glanced at the clock and saw that he was doing 1,900 kph and was at a height of 99,000 metres.

'Good Lord!' he exclaimed.

A calm voice at his elbow said: 'Yes, my son?'

73

Today's weather: A depression will mope across Southern England.

Mrs Enid Drucilla Potts, 81, of Rennison Drive, dined this week at her home. Service and cremation will be held next Thursday at 2.30 pm.

The Council have announced that they are going to cut down on unnecessary postage expenditure by asking all householders to collect their own rates bill. They will be writing to every householder this week to inform them of this fact.

Mr Horace Pulford suffered a stroke on 26 November but with the loving care of his family and his kind and efficient nurse, he never fully recovered.

ERRORS: No responsibility can be accepted for losses arising from typographical errors. Advertisers are expected to check their smalls to ensure correct appearance.

THREE BATTERED IN FISH SHOP. MAN GAOLED FOR ASSAULT.

In a bitterly cold wind, the Queen, wearing a warm sage-green tweed coat with a beaver lamb collar and a green mitre-installation of turbo-alternators and boilers.

A set of traffic lights has been stolen from a main road junction in Colchester. A police spokesman said: 'Some thieves will stop at nothing.'

Never throw away old chicken bones, or those left over from a roast. Put them in water and boil them for several hours with a few diced vegetables and a little stock, and it will make very delicious soap.

Mrs Watkins was married before anaesthetics came into use in surgical operating.

The new hospital extension will enable patients to be prepared and served in a way that has previously been impossible.

Ice cream vendors, expecting big earnings in the next few days, have arranged for huge socks to be supplied to the city.

Recently Mrs Boswell acquired a cow, and she is now supplying the whole neighbourhood with butter, milk and eggs.

We note with regret that Mr Jasper Unction is recovering from a car accident.

Before Miss Colverson concluded the concert with her rendition of 'At the end of a perfect day', she was prevented with a large bouquet of carnations from the mayoress.

The service was held at 11.00 am by the Rev. Nicholas Elsom, whose theme was 'The Evil Member in the Church'. The choir sang the anthem 'Who can it be?'.

A body was found handless, headless and bound yesterday. Police suspect foul play.

Unless teachers receive the salary increase they demand they have threatened to leave their pests.

The Prime Minister announced today that the campaign had been a hug success.

At the Women's Institute slide show the ladies included their husbands and children in their potluck supper.

The bride was dressed in a white silk and lace dress that fell to the floor. The colour scheme of the bridesmaids' dresses and flowers was punk.

Today's weather: A depression will mope across Southern England.

Colonel Monswell, the bottle scarred veteran, died at his home last Wednesday, aged 92.

Over 150 children took advantage of the mobile clinic and were examined for tuberculosis and other diseases which the clinic offered free of charge.

Mrs Nelly Mitson said that previously the neighbourhood had been a quiet area with only children and dogs riding bicycles.

Two men were admitted to hospital suffering from mild buns.

Man is found fatally murdered. His dead body was discovered in a graveyard.

The new bride over the river is approximately eighteen feet wide from buttress to buttress.

We apologize for the error in last week's paper in which we stated that Mr Charles Logworthy was a defective in the police force. This was a typographical error. We meant, of course, that Mr Logworthy is a detective in the police farce, and we apologize for any embarrassment caused.

The ladies of the Helping Hand Society enjoyed a swap social on Friday evening. Everybody brought along something that they no longer needed. Many ladies were accompanied by their husbands.

CONFUCIUS HE SAY

I'm sure you've heard people begin jokes with 'Confucius, he say...', but do you know who Confucius was? Well, he did really exist. He lived some 1,500 years ago in China. He was a very wise man, which is why his sayings have survived for such a long time. Of course, over the years the sayings have been changed quite a lot and are not always what Confucius intended...

CONFUCIUS HE SAY . . .

.... A friend in need is a pest.
.... Time is a great healer, but plastic surgery is quicker.
.... People who view the world through rose coloured glasses end up seeing red.
.... Better to keep your mouth shut and have people think you are an idiot than open your mouth and remove all doubt.
.... Frogman who jogs in still waters runs deep.
.... To err is human – so is covering it up.
.... Wine and cheese age gracefully, people don't.
.... No legs are so short they won't reach the ground.
.... It is better to have loved a short girl than never have loved a tall.
.... Never climb the ladder of success when there is a lift available.
.... Life is like a shower – one wrong turn and you're in hot water.
.... You can take a horse to water, but if you can get him to water ski you've *really* got something!
.... Man with feet planted firmly on the ground gets dirty feet.
.... Time and tide wait for no man. Neither do trains or buses.

.... He who laughs last doesn't get the joke.
.... You can fool some of the people all of the time, and all of the people some of the time – but for the rest of the time they will make fools of themselves.
.... Man who speaks with forked tongue is a snake in the grass.
.... No artist is so bad he can't draw breath.
.... Do unto others before they get a chance to do it unto you.
.... One good turn gets most of the blanket.
.... An apple a day keeps the doctor away – if thrown in the right direction.
.... Early to bed and early to rise means you never see anyone else.
.... He who finds fault with his friends has faulty friends.
.... Who say I say all those things they say I say?

THE DAFFY DICTIONARY

A

ACCORD – Thick piece of string.

ACQUAINTANCE – Someone you know well enough to borrow from but not to lend to.

ADDRESS – Something worn by girls.

ADORE – Entrance to a house.

ATTACK – A small nail.

B

BIRDHOUSE – Home tweet home.

BORE – Man who has nothing to say and says it.

BIGAMIST – Someone who makes the same mistake twice.

C

CANNIBAL – Someone who is fed up with people.

CLOAK – Sound made by a Chinese frog.

COCONUT – Someone who is mad about chocolate.

CRIMINAL – One who gets caught.

D

DEAD RINGER – Disconnected telephone.

DENIAL – Egyptian river.

DIPLOMACY – Doing nasty things in a nice way.

DIVINE – Where grapes grow.

E

ECLIPSE – What a gardener does with a hedge.

ENGINEERS – What engines hear with.

EXTINCT – Dead skunk.

F

FLEA – Insect that has gone to the dogs.

FIREPROOF – The boss's relatives.

FISSION – What scientists eat with chips.

FOUL LANGUAGE – Swearing chickens.

G

GALLOWS – Where no noose is good noose.

GOOD MANNERS – The noise you don't make when you eat your soup.

GOOSE – Bird that grows down as it grows up.

GUILLOTINE – Something that gives you a pain in the neck.

H

HALLOW – What you say when you greet someone.

HATCHET – What a hen does with an egg.

I

ICE CREAM – Yell at the top of your voice.

ILLEGAL – Sick bird.

J

JAIL – Free accommodation.

JITTERBUG – Nervous insect.

JARGON – Missing container.

JUMP – Last word in aeroplanes.

K

KIDNAP – What a baby has after lunch.

KNOB – Something to adore.

L

LIFT ATTENDANT – Person who has his ups and downs.

LISP – When you call a spade a thpade.

LAWSUIT – What a policeman wears.

LAUNCH – Meal for astronauts.

M

MOONBEAMS – What holds the moon up.

MOUSTACHE – Soup strainer.

N

NIGHTINGALE – Windy evening.

NORMALISE – Good vision.

O

OHM – Where you live.

OUCH – Sound made by two porcupines kissing.

OYSTER – What you shout when you want someone to lift up your mother.

P

PARADOX – Two doctors.

PASTEURISE – Beyond what you can see.

PRINTER – Man of letters.

Q

QUACK – Doctor who treats sick ducks.

QUARTZ – Four to the gallon.

R

REFUSE – What you do when the lights go out.

RESEARCH – Looking for something twice.

RHUBARB – Embarrassed celery.

RIVER BANK – Where fish keep their money.

S

SAGO – How you start a pudding race.

SANDWICH – Attempt to make both ends meat.

T

TORTOISE – What the teacher did.

TREASON – Male offspring of a tree.

TURTLE – Lizard with a mobile home.

U

UNAWARE – What you put on first.

UNIT – Term of abuse.

URCHIN – Lower part of a girl's face.

V

VICIOUS CIRCLE – A round geometrical figure with a nasty temper.

VESTRY – A room where vests are kept.

W

WATER – Thirst aid.

WITCHCRAFT – Flying broomstick.

X

X – What hens lay.

X-RAY – Belly vision.

Y

YANK – American dentist.

YEAR – What you hear with.

I KARNT SPEL!

Z

ZEBRA – Horse with Venetian blinds.

ZING – What you do with a zong.

ZUB – The noise made by a bee flying backwards.

Verse – and Worse

A charming young singer named Hannah,
Got caught in a flood in Savannah;
　As she floated away,
　Her sister – they say –
Accompanied her on the Piannah!

It's easy enough to be pleasant
When life flows round and round,
　But the man worth while
　Is the man who can smile
With his trousers falling down!

Down the street his funeral goes
As sobs and wails diminish,
He died from drinking varnish,
But he had a lovely finish.

Little Jack Horner sat in a corner
Eating his Christmas pie.
He put in his thumb, but instead of a plum,
He squirted fruit juice in his eye.

Some say that fleas are black,
But I know that's not so,
'Cos Mary had a little lamb
With fleas as white as snow.

A painter who lived in West Ditting
Interrupted two girls with their knitting.
　He said with a sigh,
　'That park bench – Well I
Just painted it, right where you're sitting!'

When I die, bury me deep,
Bury my history book at my feet.
Tell the teacher I've gone to rest,
And won't be back for the history test.

Here I sit in the moonlight,
Abandoned by women and men,
Muttering over and over,
'I'll never eat garlic again.'

I shot an arrow in the air
It fell to earth, I know not where.
I lose all my arrows that way.

WHO IS YELLOW, TASTES OF ALMONDS AND SWINGS FROM CAKE TO CAKE?

I DON'T KNOW—WHO?

TARZIPAN!

THE PLANNED TUG OF WAR BETWEEN ENGLAND AND FRANCE HAS HAD TO BE CANCELLED — THEY CAN'T FIND A ROPE 26 MILES LONG.

WHY DID THE SAILOR GRAB A BAR OF SOAP WHEN THE SHIP SANK?

I DON'T KNOW—WHY?

TO WASH HIMSELF ASHORE!

WHO LIES AT THE BOTTOM OF THE SEA AND IS DANGEROUS TO MAN?

I DON'T KNOW, WHO?

BILLY THE SQUID!

I'M ON THE TRAIL OF A CAT BURGLAR!

HOW DO YOU KNOW IT WAS A CAT BURGLAR?

ALL IT STOLE WAS A PINT OF MILK AND A SAUCER!

HOW MANY EARS HAS CAPTAIN KIRK GOT?

A RIGHT EAR, A LEFT EAR, AND A FINAL FRONTIER!

THE BIONIC MAN WAS STOPPED AT 165 KPH ON THE M1 — HE WAS FINED £50 AND DISMANTLED FOR 6 MONTHS.

WHEN THE ROBOT RAN OUT OF ELECTRICITY HE SAID AC COME AC GO!

WHAT DO YOU CALL A MONSTER THAT WEIGHS TWENTY TONNES AND HAS THREE HEADS?
SIR!
WHY ARE VAMPIRES CRAZY?
BECAUSE THEY ARE OFTEN BATS!
WHAT JEWELS DO MONSTERS WEAR?
TOMB STONES!
WHAT HAPPENS WHEN MONSTERS HOLD A BEAUTY CONTEST?
NOBODY WINS!
WHY DID THE MONSTER GIVE UP BOXING?
HE DIDN'T WANT TO SPOIL HIS LOOKS!
HURRY UP WITH MY SUPPER!
OH, BE QUIET! I'VE ONLY GOT THREE PAIRS OF HANDS!
WHY DON'T YOU GO OUT AND PLAY WITH YOUR BROTHER?
I'M FED UP WITH KICKING HIM AROUND!
WHAT DO MONSTERS DO WITH OLD CANNON BALLS?
PLAY MARBLES!

WHAT DID THE WOLF-MAN EAT AFTER HE HAD HIS TEETH TAKEN OUT?
THE DENTIST!
HOW DID FRANKENSTEIN EAT HIS FOOD?
HE BOLTED IT DOWN!
WHEN I GOT ON THE SCALES THIS MORNING I WEIGHED ELEVEN KILOS!
THEY CAN'T BE VERY ACCURATE!
YES THEY ARE - ALL I HAD TO ALLOW FOR WAS THE FACT THAT THE NEEDLE HAD ALREADY GONE ROUND ONCE!
WHY IS THE DRACULA FAMILY SO CLOSE?
BECAUSE BLOOD IS THICKER THAN WATER!
WHAT ANIMAL WOULD YOU PUT IN A WASHING MACHINE?
A WASH-AND-WERE-WOLF!
WHAT DID THE MONSTER SAY WHEN HE SAW SANTA CLAUS?
YUM, YUM!
WHO HAS FEATHERS, FANGS AND GOES QUACK?
COUNT DUCKULA!
DID YOU HEAR ABOUT THE GIRL MONSTER WHO WASN'T PRETTY AND WASN'T UGLY?
SHE WAS PRETTY UGLY!
WHAT IS BIG AND GREEN AND SITS IN THE CORNER ALL DAY?
THE INCREDIBLE SULK!
WHAT DOES A MONSTER DO WHEN HE LOSES A HAND?
GOES TO A SECOND-HAND SHOP!

CRAZY PUZZLES

Look at the puzzles very carefully before you attempt them. They aren't easy and your eyes and brain may deceive you. The time limit for all ten puzzles is six hours. Good luck!

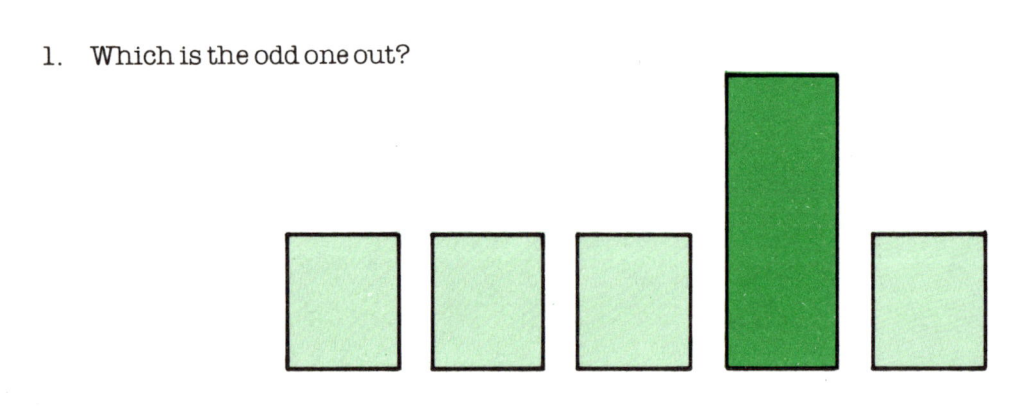

1. Which is the odd one out?

2. Which shape goes in which hole?

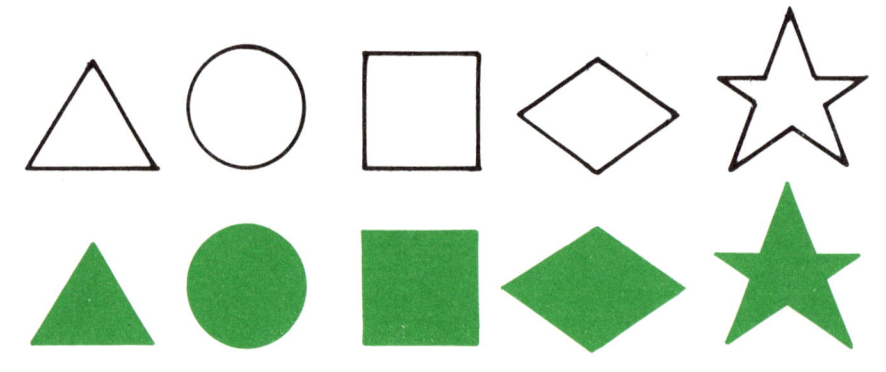

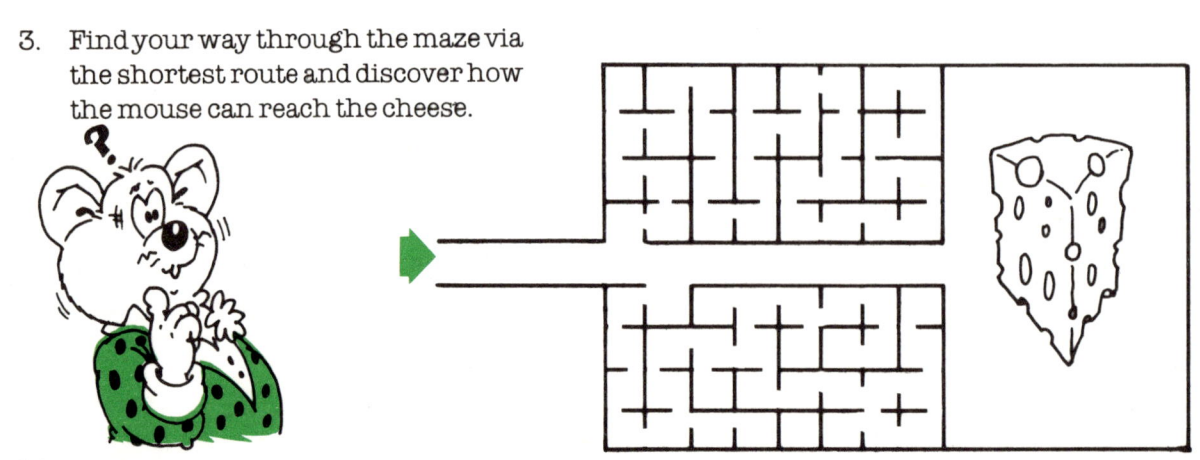

3. Find your way through the maze via the shortest route and discover how the mouse can reach the cheese.

4. Join the dots and see what shape you get.

5. Which of the following sums are wrong?
   a) $2 + 2 = 6$
   b) $100 - 100 = 100$
   c) $3 + 3 + 3 - 3 - 3 - 3 = 0$
   d) $1 + 1 - 8 = 99$
   e) $½ + ½ = 1$
   f) $2 + 3 = 9,108,677$
   g) $1,000 + 14,000 = 16$
   h) $0 + 0 = 0$

6. Which is the biggest slice of cheese?

7. What does this message in invisible ink say?

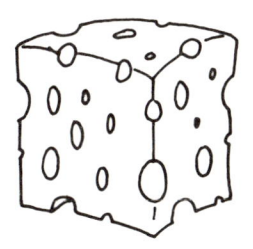

8. How many words can you make out of the words
   C H O C O L A T E   M O U S E ?

   Here are a few to start you off:
   Mouse, Chocolate, Late, Choco, Mouch, Chlouse, Scomlot, Emouscolate...

9. Spot TEN differences between these two pictures:

10. Is a baby hippo called a Nappy-potomouse?

    Please draw your answer to this question very carefully.

WAITER, WAITER!

'We have practically everything on the menu, sir.'
'So I see. Bring me a clean one.'

'Waiter, waiter, you've got your thumb in my soup.'
'Don't worry, sir, it's not hot.'

'Waiter, waiter, there's a fly in my soup.'
'Hang on a minute, I'll call the RSPCA.'

'Waiter, waiter, what is this soup?'
'It's bean soup, sir.'
'I don't care what it's been. What is it now?'

'Waiter, waiter, there's a dead beetle in my wine.'
'You asked for something with a little body in it.'

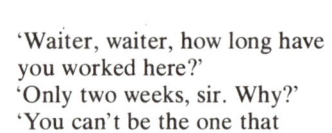

'Waiter, waiter, how long have you worked here?'
'Only two weeks, sir. Why?'
'You can't be the one that took my order then.'

'Waiter, waiter, now you've got your thumb on my steak!'
'Well, I don't want to drop it on the floor again.'

'Waiter, waiter, this lobster's only got one claw.'
'It's been in a fight, sir.'
'Well, bring me the winner then.'

'Waiter, waiter, will my pancakes be long?'
'No, they'll be round, sir.'

'Waiter, waiter, this coffee's weak!'
'What do you expect me to do, give it weight training?'

BELT UP!
MY BONNET LIES OVER THE OCEAN
OUCH!
MY FIAT IS KILLING ME
LET'S NOT MEET BY ACCIDENT
JIM COULDN'T FIX THIS
MY HUSBAND AND I
I WAS A ROLLS-ROYCE BEFORE MY ACCIDENT
I HATE CAR STICKERS!
CAR STICKERS IMPROVE YOUR HEALTH
WHEEL MEET AGAIN
WHAT'S THE HIGHWAY CODE?
THIS SIDE UP
AN OPEL FOR THE TEACHER
MY CAR IS OLD BUT IT'S IN FRONT OF YOURS AND PAID FOR
KEEP DEATH OFF THE ROAD — DRIVE ON THE PAVEMENT
THEY DON'T MAKE CARS LIKE THEY AUTO

I'M GOING TO SING MY FAVOURITE SONG!
WHAT'S THAT?
'FANGS FOR THE MEMORY'
OH, YOU'RE A PAIN IN THE NECK!
WE'RE GOING ON HOLIDAY TOMORROW – REMIND ME TO CANCEL THE DAILY PINT OF BLOOD!
WE'RE STAYING AT OUR FAVOURITE GHOST-HOUSE!
I'VE GOT TO GO INTO HOSPITAL.
WHAT FOR?
TO HAVE MY GHOUL STONES REMOVED!
IF WE HAD ANY GUTS WE'D GET OUT OF HERE!
YES, BUT WE'VE GOT NO BODY TO TAKE US!
WHY DO GHOSTS ALWAYS LIE PERFECTLY FLAT WHEN THEY SLEEP?
I EXPECT THEY USE A SPIRIT-LEVEL!
I'VE GOT A BAD COUGH!
HAVE SOME OF MY COFFIN DROPS!
I KEEP WALKING INTO THINGS – I MUST GET SOME SPOOKTACLES!
IS IT THE WITCHING HOUR YET?
I DON'T KNOW. I'VE LOST MY WITCH-WATCH!

WHAT DO YOU CALL A SPIRIT THAT WALKS BACKWARDS THROUGH WALLS AND GOES 'ER... BOO'?
COME ON, SON, WE'RE GOING TO TAKE YOU TO A PHANTOMIME!
FANGS VERY MUCH, DEAD, IS MUMMY COMING TOO?
NO, SHE'S GONE TO BUY SOME TOMBSTONES!
SOUNDS LIKE A NERVOUS GHOST TO ME!
WHAT'S A VAMPIRE'S FAVOURITE DANCE?
ISN'T IT A FANGDANGO?
WHAT DO YOU CALL A GHOST DOCTOR?
A SURGICAL SPIRIT!
I DON'T BELIEVE IN GHOSTS!
I DON'T KNOW ABOUT YOU, BUT I DON'T SEEM TO FRIGHTEN PEOPLE ANY MORE!
I KNOW! WE MIGHT AS WELL BE DEAD FOR ALL THEY CARE!
MUM, WHAT'S FOR SUPPER?
GHOULASH! NOW BE QUIET AND ONLY SPOOK WHEN YOU ARE SPOOKEN TO!
I'M OFF MY HEAD!

Top Shelf

- THE FLOWER GARDEN — Polly Anthus
- THE SPICY SAUSAGE — Della Katessen
- GROW YOUR OWN VEGETABLES — Rosa Carrots
- ACHES AND PAINS — Arthur Ritis
- AT THE SOUTH POLE — Anne Tarctic
- HOW TO FEED ELEPHANTS — P. Nuts
- HOW TO APOLOGISE — Thayer Thorry
- THE BARBER OF SEVILLE — Aaron Floor
- HOW TO MAKE AN IGLOO — S. K. Mow
- ALL ABOARD THE SHIP — Abel Seamann
- WHAT'S UP, DOC? — Howie Dewin
- SCHOOL DINNERS — R. E. Volting
- HOW TO GET THERE — Ridya Bike
- THE NAUGHTY SCHOOLBOY — Enid Spanking
- WHO KILLED CAIN — Howard I. Know

Middle Shelf

- JUSTICE OF THE PEACE
- ECONOMIC BREAKFAST — Roland Marge
- ROUND THE MOUNTAIN — Sheila B. Cummin
- WINNING ON THE FRUIT MACHINE — Jack Potts
- ONE HUNDRED YARDS TO THE BUS STOP — Willy Makitt, illustrated by Betty Wont
- THE WORKING OF AN ELECTRIC DRILL — Andy Gadget
- END OF THE WEEK — Gladys Friday
- LOOKING FORWARD — Felix Ited
- THE CALYPSO BAND — Lydia Dustbin
- WINNING ON THE FRUIT MACHINE — Jack Potts
- DON'T GIVE UP — Percy Vere
- THE MILLIONAIRE — Ivor Fortune
- THE WORLD OF VEGETABLES — R. T. Choke
- HIT ON HEAD — I. C. Stars

Bottom Shelf

- THE POST-SCRIPT — Adeline Extra
- KEEPING CHEERFUL — Mona Lott
- HORROR STORIES — R. U. Scared
- THE COWS ESCAPE — Gay Topen
- THE OPEN GATE — Wanda Off
- THE UGLY HAG — Ida Face
- THE INSOMNIAC — Eliza Wake
- THE LOST BET — Henrietta Hatt
- I'VE BEEN BITTEN — A. Flea
- THE EMBARRASSING MOMENT — Lucy Lastic
- THE NEW DRUM — Major Headache
- NOISY NIGHTS — Constance Norah
- PUNISHED SCHOOLBOY — Major Bumsaw
- FOOD ON THE PLATE — E. Tittup

THE 100 WORST JOKES IN THE HISTORY OF THE WORLD

100 Why is it nice being a baby?
It's a nappy time.

99 What cake is dangerous?
Attila the Bun.

98 PETER: Can you tell me the way to Bath?
PAUL: I always use soap and water.

97 'I bought this new camel coat.'
'It looks as if the camel's still in it.'

96 Who gets the sack as soon as he starts work?
The postman.

95 'Waiter, do you call this a three-course meal?'
'Yes, sir, two chips and a pea.'

94 What happens if you dial 666?
An Australian policeman arrives.

93 'Here, what have I got in my hands?'
'A horse and cart.'
'You peeped!'

92 When should a mouse carry an umbrella?
When it's raining cats and dogs.

91 A man asks a butcher: 'Have you a sheep's head?' 'No, sir,' says the butcher, 'it's just the way I part my hair.'

90 How can you avoid falling hair?
Jump out of the way.

89 JUDGE: Why did you hit the dentist?
MAN: Because he got on my nerves.

88 'My dentist comes from abroad.'
'Oh, he's of foreign extraction then.'

87 Why did the daft man like to be by himself?
Because he preferred to be a loon.

86 What do you get if you cross a policeman with a telegram?
Copper wire.

85 What was the most difficult thing for a knight in armour to do?
Scratch himself.

84 What bird starts out with two legs and ends up on four?
A turkey, it ends up on the table.

83 'Why does your dad take you to school?'
'He has to. We're in the same class.'

82 Why did the ant elope?
Nobody Gnu.

81 What are musicians supposed to wear?
Cords.

80 How does a motorist get a sheep to look round?
He makes a ewe turn.

79 Why did the boy take an axe to school?
It was breaking up day.

78 What did the idiot call his pet tiger?
Spot.

77 What is black, out of its mind and sits in trees?
A raven lunatic.

91

76 Why are cabbages generous?
They have big hearts.

75 Did you hear about the man who was so henpecked that his wife wouldn't let him talk in his sleep?

74 What do you get if you cross a policeman with an octopus?
A cop with eight long arms of the law.

73 When is a fountain like a biscuit tin?
When it's a square tin!

72 How did the midget get into the police force?
He lied about his height.

71 Why was the football team called The Scrambled Eggs?
Because they were always beaten.

70 What did the five-hundred kilo mouse say when it walked into the alley?
Here kitty, kitty.

69 What do cats strive for?
Purr-fection.

68 What did one toe say to the other toe?
Look out, two heels are following us.

67 What is a big game hunter?
A man who loses his way to the football match.

66 What bird is always out of breath?
A puffin.

65 What is horse sense?
Just stable thinking.

64 'I asked my husband for a fur this Christmas. He just scraped some out of the kettle.'

63 Why did the robot go mad?
Because he had a screw loose.

62 What makes people shy?
Coconuts.

61 What do you get if you cross a telephone with a gun dog?
A golden receiver.

60 What is the best place for water skiing?
A lake with a slope.

59 What tree can't you climb?
A laboratory.

58 MOTHER: What do you want to do when you're as big as your father?
SON: Go on a diet.

57 What is a meatball?
A dance in a butcher's shop.

56 What do punks learn at school?
Punktuation.

55 What is the quickest way to the station?
Run like mad.

54 What is ten metres tall, green with blue feet, and sings like a canary?
Nothing.

53 What was the baby bear who was born bald called?
Fred Bear.

52 What do you call a kindhearted, neat and handsome monster?
A failure.

51 Where did Noah keep his bees?
In archives.

50 Young photographer to model: 'Well, don't just stand there, get in focus.'

49 What is the expression on an auctioneer's face?
For bidding.

48 TEACHER: What is garlic?
LILLIE: It's the sort of language Scotsmen speak.

47 What is a Greek cat's favourite food?
Mouse-aka.

46 What sort of meat do simpletons like?
Chump chops.

45 I have five noses, three eyes, and seven ears. What am I?
Very ugly.

44 How should you dress on a very cold day?
Quickly.

43 Boy to policeman: 'Send for the Flying Squad, I've lost my budgie.'

42 How was spaghetti invented?
Someone used his noodle.

41 Tyres hold up cars. What holds up an aeroplane?
Hijackers.

40 HUSBAND: You're always wishing for things you haven't got.
WIFE: What else is there to wish for?

39 What did the dirt say when it rained?
If this keeps up my name will be mud.

38 The trouble with cannibal jokes is that they aren't in good taste.

37 Did you hear about the pig who took a plane ride?
Swine 'flu.

36 Where do cows go when they want a night out?
They go to the mooooovies.

35 MRS C: Any news about Elsie?
MRS D: No, I've told you more than I know already.

34 What do you call a Welsh apple?
A Taffy apple.

33 Why have African elephants got big ears? Because Noddy won't pay them the ransom.

32 What made the bed spread?
It saw the pillow slip.

31 What do disc jockeys wear?
A track suit.

30 'Do you know anyone who's been on the telly?'
'My dog, but he's housetrained now.'

29 Why are fat people important?
Because they carry a lot of weight.

28 'Doctor, doctor, I feel like a bar of soap.'
'That's life, boy.'

27 What makes the Tower of Pisa lean?
Because it never eats.

26 Why did the fish blush?
Because the sea weed.

25 What is a three-season bed?
One without a spring.

24 When is a black dog not a black dog?
When it's a grey hound.

23 Who tracks down lost vicars?
The Bureau of Missing Parsons.

22 What do you give a seasick elephant?
Plenty of room!

21 What animal drives a car?
A road hog.

20 What sugar sings?
Icing sugar.

19 Why did the little ink-spots cry?
Because their mother was in the pen doing a long sentence.

18 What do angry mice send each other at Christmas?
Cross-mouse cards.

17 Where was Solomon's temple?
At the side of his head.

16 What do bees say in summer?
'Swarm.'

15 Why is a busy church bell like an old joke?
Because it is always being tolled.

14 How did the gardener make his tomatoes red?
He kept saying rude things to them.

13 MAN: Hey, why are you in the tree?
BOY: Well, your sign says keep off the grass.

12 1st SECRETARY: Do you file your nails?
2nd: No, I just throw them away.

11 Yesterday was Harold's birthday and he sent a telegram of congratulations to his mother.

10 JUDGE: You have been acquitted of bigamy and can go home to your wife.
MR B: Thanks, but which one?

9 Why was the cat small?
Someone fed him condensed milk.

8 DOGS TO BE CARRIED ON THE ESCALATOR
That must be difficult in peke hour!

7 'I had to shoot my dog.'
'Was he mad?'
'Well, he wasn't too pleased about it.'

6 'I feed my dog onions every day.'
'Why do you do that?'
'It makes his bark worse than his bite.'

5 Have you heard they are now building burglarproof houses?
They're calling them Sure Lock Homes.

4 Why are tall people lazy?
Because they lie longer in bed.

3 Scent manufacturers are people who push their business into other people's noses.

2 If a husky dog can stand the lowest temperatures, which can stand the highest? A hot dog.

1 What's black and white and red all over?
It must be *The Madcap Giant Book of Jokes*.
It's in black and white – and it's read all over the world!

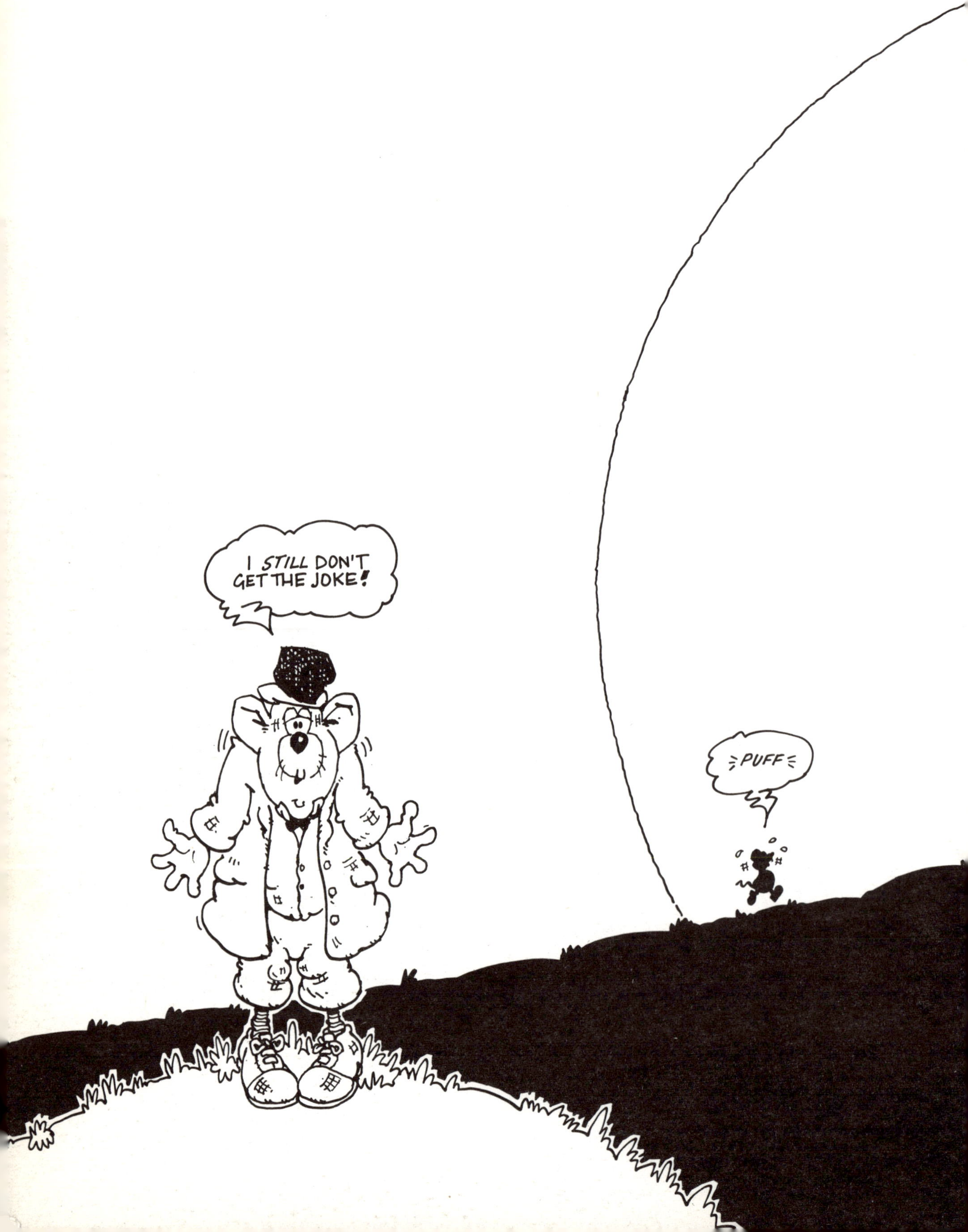
I STILL DON'T GET THE JOKE!
PUFF

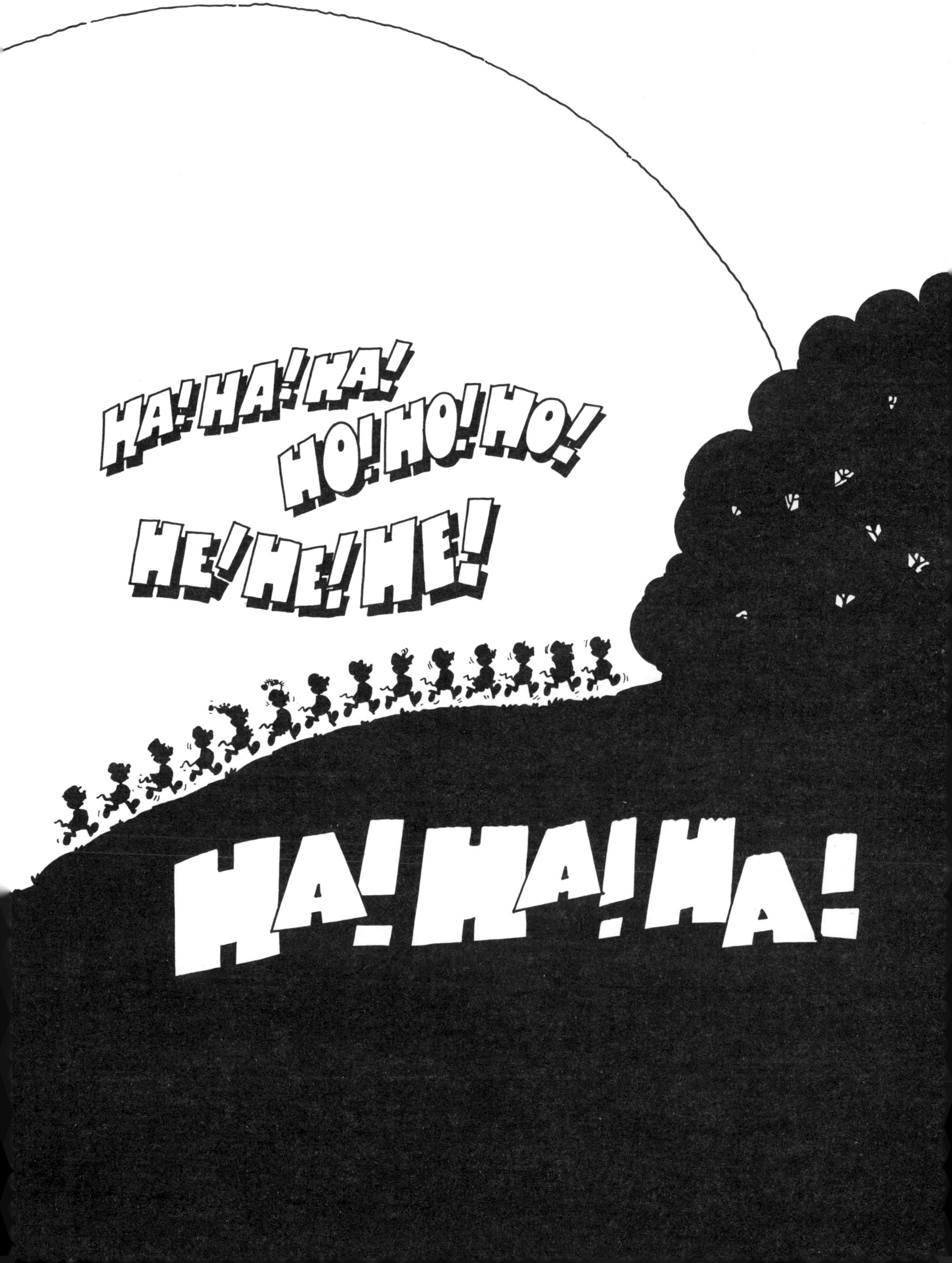
HA! HA! HA!
HO! HO! HO!
HE! HE! HE!
HA! HA! HA!